Holland and the Hollanders

The Netherlands, the small, flat country at the north-western tip of the European Continent is also known as Holland and, historically, the Lowlands, based on the fact that a substantial part of the country lies below sea level. The people of the Netherlands are known as the Dutch and historically as the Hollanders and the Lowlanders. Holland may be a small country, but it is extremely diverse. Put another way, the only natural features that Holland misses are mountains. With the exception of mountains, we have almost every other conceivable type of landscape in our country. There are pastures, heaths, forests, large rivers, lakes and islands, nature reserves and an enormous stretch of sandy coastline. In the course of its long history, those diverse landscapes have led to enormous variations in the way people lived, as well as in the use of the land. Obviously the diversity is partially due to the fact that, with-

Part I Holland...

out railways and freeways, many of the regions developed independently of one another in earlier days. The Netherlands has many typical fishing villages, which are reminiscent of its glorious seagoing tradition, windmills that were used for production purposes and to keep the land dry, agricultural land with quaint little farms, cultivated land and cows, flower farms, historical city centres, and a great deal more.

For Hetty,
Remco, Linda and Harold

Published by:

Sportmark 110
NL 1355 KH Almere
www.perfectpicture.nl

Realisation and Production: Perfect Picture
Art Direction, Text and Photography: Dirk M. de Boer
Text and Edited by: Jan Dirk de Block
Translation: A-T International Communications, Almere
Design and DTP: Vandinther Vormgevers, Bussum
Scanning and Lithography: Fritz Repro BV, Almere
Printed by: Proost NV, Turnhout

This publication may not be copied and/or published by printer, photocopier or microfilm or in any other manner without the prior written permission of the publisher or copyright holder.
All information concerning the use of photography, texts and/or related products are obtainable from Perfect Picture in Almere (NL).
Tel: +31 (0) 36-53 153 44 Fax: +31 (0) 36 53 160 52
E-mail: info@perfectpicture.nl

ISBN 90-805073-2-6
NUGI 922
EAN 9789060507313
© 2001 Perfect Picture, Almere (NL)

Dit boek is ook verkrijgbaar in het Nederlands

Nature & Nostalgia

Table of Contens

Forword
Hans van Driem
Managing Director - Netherlands Board of Tourism — 07

Introduction
D. M. de Boer - Perfect Picture — 08

Part I — Holland...

Chapter 1	Concise History	11
Chapter 2	The Weather and the Wadden Sea	27
Chapter 3	Fisheries and Shipping	39
Chapter 4	Fortesses, Strongholds, Castels and Pleasure Gardens	59
Chapter 5	Crafts	75
Chapter 6	Windmills	87

Part II — ... and the Hollanders

Chapter 7	Farms and Traditional Costumes	103
Chapter 8	Clogs and Cheese	117
Chapter 9	Agriculture, Crop Cultivation and Livestock	131
Chapter 10	Homage to the Tulip	147
Chapter 11	Flowers and Greenhouses	157
Chapter 12	Winter Festivities and Fun on the Ice	169

Nature in The Netherlands — 180

Photo explanations — 184

Tourist information — 188

Thanks — 192

Nature & Nostalgia

During the greatest Ice Age, approximately 140,000 years ago, half of Holland was covered with a layer of ice several kilometres deep. The ice moved down from Scandinavia and shaped the hills in the provinces of Overijssel, Gelderland and Utrecht. All our hills and ridges were shaped by the moraine that was formed at the edges of the ice sheets after they had melted. The moraines moved down from areas such as the Scandinavian mountains. The ice layer had craggy shapes full of fissures and cracks not unlike Alpine glaciers. The soil was permanently frozen, as prevailing temperatures were comparable to those currently prevalent around the poles.

Forword

Every facet of our beautiful country is depicted in this unique book by Dirk M. de Boer. With it he has succeeded in creating a truly breathtaking presentation of the Netherlands. His depiction of the country also coincides perfectly with those places to which the Netherlands Board of Tourism generally attracts foreign tourists. The author has managed to create a vision of the richly varied history of our changing country from its earliest origins to contemporary times. He has brilliantly captured the seasons and related events in the country, as well as in the cities. Our stunning natural landscapes, and the water that makes its presence felt everywhere, occupy a substantial part of the book. Obviously this is important; the Netherlands is a small and crowded country, so we need to take extra care of our natural heritage and characteristic landscapes. Sustainable tourism is something that will become increasingly important in the future. Foreign tourism to the Netherlands will continue to grow as an industry in the years to come. This entails a continuing demand for striking and extraordinary publications on the Netherlands. After all, we have a lovely country and we need to tell the world about it.

Hans van Driem
Managing Director - Netherlands Board of Tourism

In winter light travels further through our atmosphere. The countless particles of light reflect the most fantastic colours and create this dreamlike light, reflected with incredible precision in the thin layer of ice on the water.

Chapter 1

Concise History

A History of 200,000 Years

The first signs of human inhabitation of the Lowlands date back some 150,000 to 200,000 years. Dating was based on discoveries of ancient tools, such as the celt. The age of such tools can be determined reasonably accurately by dating the layer of soil in which it was discovered. The celt was typically used as a knife or scraper to skin animals. During the great Ice Age, some 140,000 years ago, the sea level was approximately 50 metres lower than it is today. Due to the extreme cold, most areas of dry land, including parts of the North Sea, were permanently frozen. Land ice pushing down from Scandinavia broke the land face up into plates that were later packed into layers by the ice cap. Eventually the sheer weight of the 2.5-km ice layer re-levelled the ground. The edges of the glacial tips created ridges, which today form well-known hills, such as Gaasterland, Holterberg, Veluwe, and the Utrechtse Heuvelrug, as well as moraines in areas that are presently known as Urk and Wieringen. These are some of the locations where ancient celts are currently being discovered. Some of the large rocks carried down from Scandinavia remained behind and were used much later - approximately 5,000 years ago – to create megalithic tombs.

Ice Ages and Floods

The Ice Age was followed by a long warm period, which was followed by yet another Ice Age. In the arctic climate of approximately 50,000 years ago, the Lowlands was more than likely the hunting grounds of Neanderthal man. This ancient humanoid hunted deer, and a host of long-extinct species, such as the furry rhinoceros and the mammoth. Some time later, these short, stocky Europeans were driven away by our direct ancestor, Cro-Magnon man. Every now and then, North Sea fishermen still trawl in mammoth tusks from the bed of the North Sea, which, during the Ice Age, was a hostile tundra landscape. The last Ice Age was followed by a series of warm and cold periods; however, the Lowlands was never to be covered by glacial ice again.

The last Ice Age ended some 12,000 to 10,000 years ago. The inhabitants of the Lowlands at the end of the Ice Age were deer hunters, and samples of their tools, including stone spears and arrow tips, have been found in local diggings. Local climates became significantly more temperate after the last Ice Age, which gave rise to major changes in the local flora and fauna. The icy tundra made way for dense forests, which, in turn, led to the migration of the deer. However, as a result of the enormous volumes of melted ice in the region, large tracts of land to the north and west of the country ended up below sea level. In those days the Lowlands consisted of a jagged coastline of tidal sands and stretches of land that would have been underwater regularly due to massive flooding caused by the rivers known as the Rhine and the Maas. The Lowlands of those times would have been a hazardous homeland indeed. Moors, lakes and pools punctuated extensive stretches of reed lands. It initially consisted mostly of beech and pine trees, but later included oak, alder, elm, and lime wood trees in the drier areas. Fauna, such as elks, European bison, aurochs, wild boars and red deer yielded nutrition for human hunters who, until approximately 7,000 years ago, lived exclusively from hunting. In those days, wolves, lynx and bears also inhabited the forests.

An Insecure Existence On Rich Hunting Grounds

Recently, a number of 5,500-year old graves were discovered in the sandy hills of the former dune lands of Ypenburg. Based on those, and other discoveries, we have a fairly good idea of the nature of the environment and the lifestyles of the people that occupied the region at the time. They were hunter-gatherers who did not simply wander about aimlessly, but occupied permanent encampments. This was, at the time, a beautiful, untouched wilderness. Undoubtedly, the inhabitants lived a highly insecure existence in a region where the sea and wind played constant havoc with the dunes, and river courses changed randomly with every new flood. Continuous displacement of the sands, and thereby the coastline and regular flooding, created a highly varied landscape and ideal habitat for marine life, as well as exceptional feeding grounds

Compacted by the wind between thawing and freezing, ice can adopt bizarre and fascinating forms. The reflection of sunlight makes it even more beautiful.

Concise History

the rest could fulfil other useful tasks.

The advent of bronze (2,100 BC) and iron (700 BC) as the media of tool production were further critical points in our cultural evolution. Based on archaeological calculations it was established that, in the Iron Age, the Lowlands was populated by some 25,000 souls. Most of the above-mentioned changes occurred later in our region than they did in regions located further to the south and east of the European continent. In fact, it was immigrants from those regions that introduced most of the changes. Discoveries in local digs also indicate that a significant amount of travelling and trading took place in those days, whereby it is reasonable to deduce that exchange played an important part in man's daily existence.

The Romans in Holland

The arrival of the Romans here, in approximately 50 BC, brought about further major changes. The Roman thinker, Tacitus, first mentioned the Northern regions in his writings around the year AD 0, and described the local population as the "Barbarians of the North". Another Roman historicist, Pliny, mentioned floating islands near the coast that could yield problems for Roman vessels. The floating islands were in fact floating bogs, complete

with trees that had been separated from the land by the ocean. The first authentic Dutch text, in Ancient Dutch, was written much later by a lovesick monk in the form of a melancholy verse: "All the birds have started to nest, except you and I". It would probably have been quite hard, in those days, not to notice the overwhelming numbers of birds in the Lowlands. Roman historicists did write about the inhabitants of the Lowlands with some sympathy, and apparently found it hard to imagine that any-

Most of the lower-lying regions of the Netherlands have literally been reclaimed from the sea. Remnants of the oldest villages in the west of the country were discovered in the dunes and river deltas. Later on, prior to the advent of dike-building technology, inhabitants created terps or knolls to accommodate farms and the first settlers of new villages. The alluvial land surrounding the terps was often completely flooded. Frisian farmers still experienced this in the Middle Ages. The first small dikes were built around 1100 AD. However those smaller dikes, and even some of the later, heavier ones, offered limited resistance to the force of the surrounding waters.

Concise History 15

body would voluntarily live on a hand-made hill (terps) that were, as often as not, surrounded by the sea. The Romans, who, in fact, never bothered to occupy the Lowlands above the Rhine, built a fortified line of defence, known as the "limes", along the Rhine. Some of those fortifications developed into cities that still exist today and include Katwijk, Valkenburg, Alphen aan de Rijn, Utrecht and Nijmegen. Due to the presence of this borderline, Northern and Southern Holland continued to develop in isolation for several centuries longer. The inhabitants of the north, the Frisians, remained independent after the fall of the Roman Empire and became adept agriculturalists and active traders, including with the Romans. The well-known Germanic tribe, the Batavians, who inhabited the regions directly south of the border, in the present Betuwe, were brilliant equestrians and formidable

warriors, initially engaging their new rulers, the Romans, in battle, but later fighting side by side with the Romans in the Empire's legions. Generally speaking there is no question that the Romans brought modernisation and prosperity to the Lowlands. Sadly, those prosperous times were short-lived, as the centuries that followed brought about severe hardships; especially for local farmers.

Many of the larger lakes in Holland were formed by melting glaciers. Most of those lakes are surrounded by extensive reed lands and innumerable winding watercourses, the banks of which are covered with yellow irises, irises and buttercups. Water lilies cover the water with their floating leaves. These water lands form a perfect habitat for fish and amphibians, which, in turn, attract birds such as the cormorant and blue heron. The stork is also a common predator on these marshlands. The green toad is however not an easy prey, especially underwater or camouflaged in the green grass. On slightly higher terrain, the fertile soil is home to a wide variety of colourful species of trees and plants.

Concise History 17

The Middle Ages: Turbulent Times

The Frankish occupation of the Lowlands began in the sixth century. The Franks were constantly engaged in battle with the Frisians who, by that time, had occupied the entire North Sea coast as well as some inland areas, such as the Frisian trading post, Dorestad (Wijk bij Duurstede). Frisian control was finally broken under the reign of Charlemagne when the entire region fell under the administration of a single vast empire. In those days the Lowlands suffered bitterly under the constant assault of the Vikings from Scandinavia. To protect themselves against the Vikings, the locals built ringwalled fortresses in places such as Zeeland Middelburg and Oost-Souburg. The attacks continued well into the 10th century, when Holland became part of the German Empire.

The distant rule of the Germans gave rise to the establishment of counties, such as Holland, Zeeland and Gelre. To cope with continuous infighting between those counties, local rulers built strongholds and fortified castles. This began in the early Middle Ages, at around 500 BC, and continued for about a thousand years. The Feudal System came into being around the middle of this period when local warlords intensified the practise of building fortified castles. The cities, with their trades and guilds were products of the later Middle Ages. The first of those were the Hanseatic cities, such as Amsterdam, Deventer and Kampen, which were primarily involved in trade on the Oostzee. Many of these cities played a key role in the liberation of the region from Spain during the Eighty Year War. The Hanseatic cities and the VOC (Dutch East-India Company) also played a crucial role in the period known as Holland's Golden Age, at which time Holland became a sovereign state, albeit still without the provinces of Noord-Brabant and Limburg.

In former times the local population conducted trade in natural produce. Life was risky and insecure in those days. Life and property came under constant threat of attack from the likes of the Vikings who routinely plundered and pillaged the painstakingly produced possessions of the local population.

18 *Concise History*

The Eternal Struggle Against Water

Amidst the political toils and trade activities, the Dutch were locked in an ongoing battle against the forces of water; which continues to this day. The conquest of land from the sea began in earnest when locals began to drive piles and build dam walls around fertile meadows in Groningen and Friesland. Later (from 500 BC), the local population built terps upon which they built their farmsteads. The battle against the sea was a combined struggle to obtain arable land for agriculture (including crop cultivation and pastoral land) and for greater personal security. The farmers of the Middle Ages lived a hard and insecure existence. However, slowly but surely, the battle finally began to turn in their favour. Dike construction, understandably, had a major influence on local culture, and by the 13th century began to assume the form of a craft. With their dikes, the Hollanders continued to reclaim land from the sea; but also conquered increasingly large tracts of wilderness inland for small-scale agriculture. Countless dikes along the coast cut substantial tracts of land off from the sea, whereby saline waters soon became sweet. Dikes protected

Fortunately, our ancestors were a tough breed, and systematically learnt to exploit the fertile soil around them. They built dikes to fight off hostile tides, and made more intensive use of fertile soil in the riverbeds. However, the risk of flooding remained a constant threat; even today, there is always a chance of flooding waters breaking through a dike!

Concise History   19

Holland has countless small bridges – they are sorely needed to keep our feet dry in this watery land.

The enormous stalks and corollas of the hogweed remain standing until late winter. Every spring they return, some growing up to three metres high.

Nature & Nostalgia

Pages 24 and 25:
Unlike in the past, beaches and dunes are no longer totally subject to the relentless forces of wind and tide. Dikes and levees are designed to prevent dunes from collapsing and to protect the land beyond from being submerged by the tides.

To further reinforce the sand, rows of piles were driven into the sea, creating a welcome resting place for passing gulls.

Chapter 2

The Weather and the Wadden Sea

There are few countries where the weather is such an important conversation starter as in Holland. There is a good reason for this: In a country where the sun always shines, there would be little, if any, reason to talk about the weather. However, in a country where the weather changes not only from day to day, but several times in the course of a single day, there is sufficient cause to stay alert. The weather is a major variable in the Netherlands, which makes daily weather reports in the press, and on the radio and television indispensable. We are ruled by the weather – some people even suffer chronic depressions due, in no small part, to damp and dreary autumn climes. However, the prospect of a sunny weekend – a rare, but not impossible event - always brings cheer to the local morale. Holland is, in the final analysis, a country of low-pressure systems, umbrellas and raincoats. This is unavoidable given the damp climate created by the proximity of the North Sea and the Atlantic Ocean. The prevailing winds blow moisture off the Atlantic, which results in limited sunshine and the infamous low grey skies. Those grey expansive skies while oppressive, have also served as inspiration for many a famed Dutch painter.

Wind, Rain, and a Little Sunshine

The Netherlands is not only wet; it has a higher average rainfall than almost every other European country located further away from the sea. The frequent stormy winds blowing onto a country that is largely situated below sea level have, for thousands of years, made it a victim of the tempestuous seas. For thousands of years BC, the notion of living in the north and west of the country was almost inconceivable. Today, almost the entire coast of Holland serves as a barrier between the sea and the low lands beyond. In most instances this is an artificial barrier, such as dikes built into the sea, while the natural dunes are almost literally held together by marram grass.

Kind, Temperate Climate

The climate of the Netherlands is almost completely determined by its maritime location, specifically by the Caribbean Gulf Stream that flows directly towards the Netherlands. The relatively warm waters, which influence the air above, keep extreme cold away. Moreover, the Gulf Stream is the reason for our temperate climate. It is only excessively cold or hot in Holland when the wind blows in directly from the east. This is due to the fact that Central and Eastern Europe have a continental climate with extreme variance between summer and winter. How much fun is that? After all, when we are hit by a heat wave (at temperatures considered normal in the continental interior), there is the devil to pay. And while frost might be desirable for ice skaters, two months of continuous frost invariably throws the country completely out of balance. We are quite simply not accustomed to those conditions; moreover, I would hazard to say that, within reason, the variability of our climate is a blessing in disguise. After all, who really enjoys chronic sunshine and soaring temperatures, or endless spells of frost. Moreover, the moist and temperate climate is highly favourable for the varied forms of nature in the Netherlands.

The wind drives sand pebbles across the beach. Any unevenness, from the tiniest shell to a wooden pile could occasion the formation of a dune. This herring gull uses a wooden post as its watchtower.

A strong northwesterly wind approaching! That is to say, be warned, batten down, heavy weather's on the way. That not withstanding, seagulls and fulmars effortlessly navigate the currents of the wind, picking at anything that seems remotely edible. From the safety of the dunes, one cannot but admire the awesome power of the waves as it churns up sheets of froth that are blown across the beach. What better way to clear the cobwebs from our minds than this. In the stormy season, the skeletal frames of beach pavilions form wistful outlines along the edges of the dunes.

The Weather and the Wadden Sea

With a few exceptions, the entire coastline of the Netherlands forms a beautiful extended beach – ideal for hiking and horse riding, both of which can be done almost everywhere. Those seeking true tranquillity visit the Waddeneilanden (West Frisian Islands) or the province of Zeeland.
Others, seeking livelier spots, tend to go to resorts such as Hoek van Holland and Den Helder with their busy boulevards and windy piers, luxurious pavilions, colourful beach tents and herring stalls and, of course, the nightlife! Those who just want to strip it all off and let their hair down can do so on any of the kilometres of deserted beach along the coastline. And why not? This is just the kind of freedom the Dutch have become known for.

On the West Frisian island of Schiermonnikoog the sea still has its way with the sands. Here it is still possible to observe the fascinating process of nature forming new dunes out of old. This is one of the reasons Schiermonnikoog has been declared a National Park.

The Waddensea: A Unique Nature Area

The Waddensea, or West Frisian Sea, was formed by a row of dunes, sections of which are still visible on the West Frisian Islands, such as Texel, Terschelling and Ameland. Up until the year of our Lord, the row of dunes was more thoroughly sealed off than it is today. The Waddensea was formed between the continent and the dunes due to sedimentation of small fertile particles carried in from the North Sea but left behind by the weaker outgoing tides. This is an ongoing process, as a result of which the ground level of the Wadden area is continuously rising.

The Waddensea, the primary incubator of the North Sea's fauna, and the Dollard form a unique maritime zone, and an extremely important nature area, both nationally and internationally. It is therefore almost incomprehensible that not a single square metre of this precious area has been proclaimed a national park.

Many generations of coastal dwellers lived in harmony with the sea, and owe their very existence to the treasures of the sea and the river lands. Modern man seems to believe he no longer needs the sea, and continues to take more than he gives. Powerful multinationals, heedless of the hazards, continue to explore mineral oils on the ocean floor. As a result, the Waddensea today is the only section of ocean that can truly be described as 'untouched'. However, pressure is increasing to exploit this area too. Fortunately, the island of Schiermonnikoog has been declared a protected area. The island still has small remnants of times gone by; such as the shifting dunes whose patterns are determined by wind alone, unfettered by the constraints of manmade barriers and planted grass. Those dunes, and the natural channels winding through them, lined with grass and sea lavender, are a pleasure to behold. To a degree, here, as almost nowhere else today, it is possible to witness the untouched character of the coast of Holland as it may have been many centuries ago. Here, too, one can still encounter a seal taking a nap on a dry sandbank while scores of gulls glide by overhead; each with its own unique call. Endless beaches stretch out into infinity; white sands are sprinkled with bits of shell, of jellyfish, and squid sepia, all washed up and forgotten on the shore. Sadly, the sea's natural yield is punctuated by all-too-familiar bits of plastic and other manmade litter.

The Weather and the Wadden Sea

32 *The Weather and the Wadden Sea*

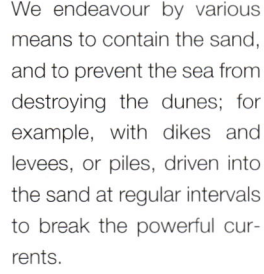

We endeavour by various means to contain the sand, and to prevent the sea from destroying the dunes; for example, with dikes and levees, or piles, driven into the sand at regular intervals to break the powerful currents.

The Weather and the Wadden Sea

Invariably, one's first hesitant steps across the dike onto the muddy flats of the West Frisian Sea or Waddenzee as it is known in Dutch, is fraught with uncertainty and doubt: Is it really possible to cross this slippery expanse? At least, that was how I experienced it. From the top of the dike the eye extends across an apparently infinite expanse of water with little wooden poles marking the edges of the dike, and a narrow passage of sediment and mud in between. I was amazed when our guide simply kept on walking, his sounding rod and walkie-talkie at the ready. After slouching through the sludge for more than half a kilometre, the only consistent thought is to get back to dry land as soon as possible. Then the guide stops and gauges the water's depth. However, all thought of a well-earned rest or waiting for the water to ebb away is soon abandoned as he plunges forth into the deep. Surely no one is going to make it to the other side. Stumbling along, you try to wash the growing layers of mud from your skin. However, slowly the water ebbs away and, before long, you are walking on firmer earth until, eventually, you find yourself safely on dry and solid seabed. To get to the island on the other side, you still need to cross a number of channels that reach chest high – swimming in a streaming channel is too dangerous. By now the dunes of Schiermonnikoog have come into view, but still you need every conscious effort to continue walking. Finally, just in time for the turning of the tide, you make it safely to the other side. In my view, a walk across the Wadden, known in Dutch as 'wadlopen' or 'Wad walking' is truly the epitome of a walk across the 'Lowlands'!

Wadlopen', An Experience not to Miss!

A unique experience that should not be missed in Holland is a walk across the bed of the Waddensea during low tide. This popular, open-air activity is known locally as 'Wadlopen', which means, literally, 'walking the Wad'. The summer tidal chart determines the schedule for these hikes, which are led by specialised guides. The starting point is the town of Pieterburen, which is also known for its seal crèche. In my personal experience, a walk across the Waddensea is the most effective way to become one with the elements that shaped, and continue to

shape, the Netherlands. This experience, and the extraordinary nature of the Wadden area will not be forgotten easily.

Every now and then, a ship or an unusual animal, such as a whale, runs aground on the coast of Holland. We do not know why whales beach here, but the prevalent theory is that they sometimes take a wrong turn into the North Sea above Scotland. In all probability they become confused by the slowly rising coast and run aground on the local beaches. Due to the enormous pressure exerted on their lungs, whales do not survive beaching. On the other hand, specialised museums are always grateful to receive new bones for their collections. In former times the carcass would remain on the beach; prey for a host of hungry scavengers. From time to time our faith in the recovery of nature is restored when, for example, a newspaper headline announces a walrus spotting near a beach in this area. Stories handed down from our great grandfathers tell of abundant marine life in this area in days gone by. However, the walrus always disappears just as unexpectedly as it appeared in the North Sea. The appearance of a walrus in our seas is a wondrous event, and one can only hope one that will be experienced somewhat more frequently by our own grandchildren.

The Weather and the Wadden Sea

In late autumn the sun breaks through the clouds and a powerful beam of light pierces the damp forest.

Large sections of the provincial roads in the Netherlands are lined with plantations. The trees were planted in long rows, and viewed from the side, they flash by row after row.

Nature & Nostalgia

Miniature eel traps are favourite collectors items. This old fisherman is hard at work keeping the supply in stock.

38 *Nature & Nostalgia*

Chapter 3

Fisheries and Shipping

A successful shipping industry can extend a small country's influence globally. In the 17th century Amsterdam was the largest staple market in Western Europe. The VOC (Dutch East India Company) was founded in 1602. It was the world's first multinational and, by the 17th century, was certainly the largest enterprise in the world. In its heyday, Europe's largest industrial complex was situated in Amsterdam on the reclaimed island of Oostburg. The scope of the complex was expressed by the size of its Large Warehouse (Het Grote Magazijn), one of many VOC warehouses in the city that measured 215 metres in length, 25 metres in width and was 4 storeys high. In addition, the port was host to shipbuilding activities and storage facilities distributed over no less than three slipways. The ropeyard building, known as the "Lijnbaan", where ship's ropes were manufactured, was no less than 500 metres long. Amsterdam was also the seat of the Admiralty that built its own battleships in several other shipyards. In the course of its 200-year existence, the VOC built a total of some 1,500 ships in four different size classes, the largest of which were over 1,000 tons while the smallest were less than 500 tons. In the 18th century, these shipyards offered daily employment to some 1,200 workers, while the total employee occupancy of the VOC in Amsterdam at the time was approximately 1,500 personnel.

Six Establishments in Holland and Zeeland

In typical Dutch tradition, the VOC was a shipping and trading enterprise that conducted trade with Asia. The company was a consolidation of a number of older companies, such as the "Compagnie van Verre", dating back to 1594, which had already begun the spice trade with Asia. The murderous competition between the companies finally forced their owners to cooperate. The cooperation was, to a great extent, stimulated by the national government of the Republic of the Seven United States of Holland (Republiek der Zeven Verenigde Hollanden). It was the famous Pensionary, Johan van Oldenbarnelvelt, who finally managed to unite the managers of the various companies around the same table.

The companies were not only based in Amsterdam, as the VOC had offices (chambers) in Hoorn, Enkhuizen, Rotterdam, Delft, Zeeland (Middelburg) and Amsterdam. Amsterdam was by far the largest chamber with twenty directors or governors against Middelburg's twelve, and seven in each of the remaining cities. The Council of the "Heren XVII" (17 Lords) that convened three times a year to determine the company's policies was formed within those chambers. The Heren XVII was the highest council in the enterprise and Amsterdam was represented by eight, Zeeland four and the other cities by one delegate each. This added up to only sixteen, as the 17th seat was occupied on a rotational basis by the four smaller chambers.

Shareholders from Every Level of Society

How was it possible to launch an enterprise that, in those days, must have required a very substantial amount of operating capital? Surprisingly, in almost exactly the same way as it is done today – by issuance, in 1602, of common shares in the company. It is very likely that the phenomenal success of the launch was due largely to a highly effective publicity campaign preceding the days of the launch. A total of more than 6.4 million guilder's worth of stock was sold - an enormous amount for that time. Of that amount, Amsterdam was allocated the lion's share of more than 3.5 million. Archive records show that citizens from every walk of local life took part: Regents and officials, lawyers, doctors, and notaries, craftsmen,

For a fisherman, the expression "There's no place like home" mostly means "There's no place like the cabin". However, there is not much time for lounging about in the cabin, as there is always something that needs to be done on a wooden ship; like scraping, painting, caulking and repairing.

Fisheries and Shipping

such as bakers, butchers, shoemakers, carpenters, coopers, grocers, wine sellers, even domestic servants. Participants bought as many shares as they could afford, which was anything between 25,000 and 50 guilders. The Amsterdam share registry shows a record of 1,143 shareholders in the first share register of the VOC.

The company's management structure was extremely modern. The Board of Governors of the chambers were divided into various commissions, each with its own designated tasks. The

While the ships of the VOC (Verenigde Oostindische Compagnie or Dutch East Indian Company) were pure works of art, life on board those ships were somewhat less than romantic – it was, in fact, rather dangerous. For example, the sheer risk of climbing the rigging to hoist the sails, or getting to the crow's nest was considerable. As were the health risks due to limited and monotonous meals with occasional measured doses of rum. Add to that the heavy disciplinary punishments, uncomfortable sleeping quarters, years away at sea, diseases, the numerous naval battles with neighbouring countries and, of course, the ever present

Auditor's Commission was charged with bookkeeping, the Commission of Revenue was, among other things, responsible for dispatching funds to Asia, the Trade Commission saw to the storage and sales of goods from the Orient, and, finally, the Equipage Commission supervised the construction, maintenance and fitting of the company's ships and the recruitment of ship's personnel, such as seamen, military personnel and traders. Ships sailed out three times a year, at Christmas, Easter and in September - always in convoy to counter piracy on the high seas.

threat of a shipwreck and drowning at sea. It was, however, this hard life that gave Holland its Golden Ages - a period during which the nation accumulated enormous wealth and which enabled the construction of stately canal houses in Amsterdam and grand mansions on the River Vecht at Utrecht.

40 *Fisheries and Shipping*

A Tough, Adventurous Life for no Money

While the company's organisation was rather modern for its time (this was still only the 17th and 18th centuries), recruitment was somewhat different from today. This was particularly true for those who were most at risk - the seamen and soldiers, the latter of whom served primarily in the VOC trading regions of Asia. Whether risky or not, the enthusiasm for a job in the VOC was substantial, as, along with the extraordinary dose of adventure, the ambitious could look forward to reasonably rapid promotion and the more enterprising among them could make a good living out of a bit of smuggling on the side. Smuggling was, in fact, almost essential, as wages were rather low. An able seaman rarely earned much more than 7 to 11 guilders a month; with a third mate pocketing approximately 26 guilders a month. That notwithstanding, it was not always easy to recruit workers in such a thriving economy. As a result, it was sometimes necessary to import workers, mostly soldiers, from Germany and Scandinavia. In the 18th century, no less than half of all personnel hailed from those regions. Some incredible tales relate how the VOC bought entire regiments of soldiers from impoverished German rulers. For example, the Duke of Württemberg provided the company with no less than 2,200 soldiers in return for three tons of gold. The Württemberg regiment eventually embarked from Middelburg for an uncertain future in Asia. And uncertain it most certainly was; the outward-bound journey lasted eight months (each ship was away from its home port for two years), and all rations on board were dried, canned or pickled. The dry ship's biscuits were almost as famous as scurvy was infamous due to the short supply of fresh nutrition.

Fisheries and Shipping

Survival was a Matter of Luck

While the Cape of Good Hope, approximately halfway to Asia, offered fresh food and drink, every ship was more or less guaranteed to loose one third of its crew to diseases such as dysentery, bubonic plague ('rotkoorts'), varicose veins ('blauwscheut') and typhus. In India the crew could expect to contract dysentery and a host of related diseases from local foods. All this was over and above the many combat related mortalities. Moreover, many seamen died en route due to host of unsavoury punitary measures, such as flogging, branding, or being 'nailed to the mast', none of which the victim was very likely to survive. These punishments were meted out for a host of petty, punishable misdemeanours. However, those who did survive the aforementioned treatment were very unlikely to survive a keelhauling. Compared to the punishment inflicted on board, shipwrecking was a minor risk – only three percent of all VOC ships were actually wrecked.

Further food for thought: At that time, in the homeland, the average life expectancy was not much more than 40 years. Nevertheless, by the time a VOC ship returned to Holland or Zeeland, it was rare for more than one third of the original crew be on board. A consideration in that regard was the fact that many of the seamen settled in Asia, while many soldiers remained behind to guard numerous VOC trading posts. Around 1750, the company employed nearly 25,000 people in the Far East, including soldiers and traders seeking Asian merchandise to sell in the homeland. The enormous operating expenses, in conjunction with the cost of the war against the English, who reigned over the sea during the 18th century, led to the company's bankruptcy, and ultimately, to the suspension of the VOC on 31 December 1799.

The company brought enormous wealth to Holland; not only the traders in oriental goods accumulated wealth, but beneficiaries included supply companies, such as importers and suppliers of wood, tar, iron, and hemp used in the shipping industry. Other beneficiaries were the suppliers of food and clothing, and retailers who sold the spices, tea, coffee, Chinese earthenware and textiles to the public. In short, our Golden Age largely owed its existence to the VOC.

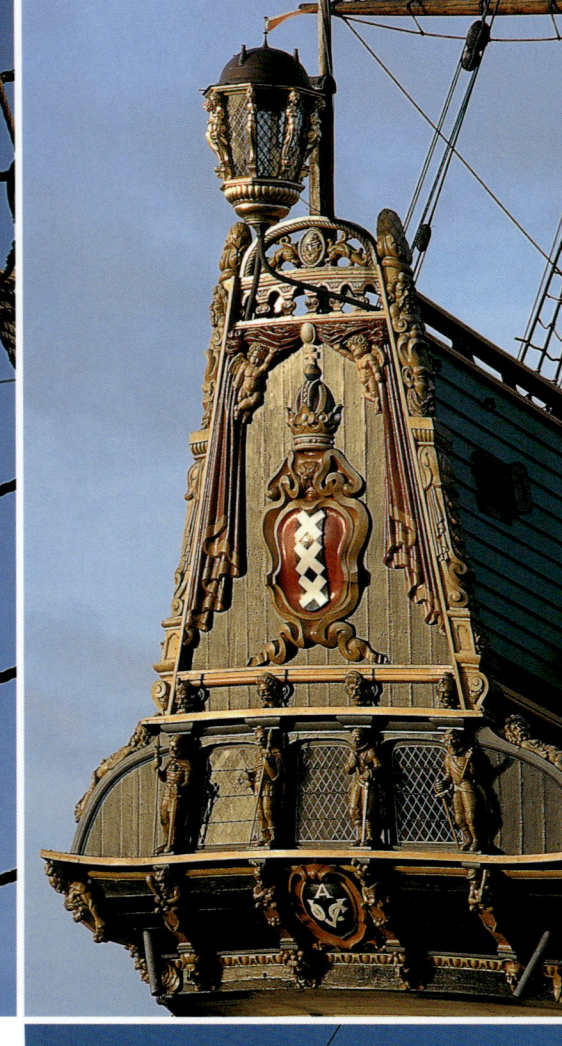

The Dutch flag dates back to the 16th century (the time of William of Orange), making it one of the oldest national flags in the world. Sadly, the lovely orange colour was later replaced with red (Dutch national sports teams still wear orange in their outfits).

There were shipyards in many ports, the largest of which were in Amsterdam. In the year 1600, one of the ships built in Amsterdam, "De Liefde" (Love), landed in Usuki Bay in Japan. This established the initial contact with Japan and, from 1641, Holland was the only country permitted to conduct trade with Japan. Until 1854, the Dutch continued to conduct exclusive trade with Japan from their trading post on the small island of Desjima in Nagasaki. A VOC ship was an industry in itself with a rigid hierarchy, reaching up to the captain, who was the lord and master of his domain.

Fisheries and Shipping

Pages 44 and 45:
The sea provides food, but also hazards. The dike forms the only protection against the water and is therefore still high enough to catch sufficient wind to dry the nets.

Harvests from the sea and rivers determine the diet of the Dutch seafood lover: Herring, flounder, eel, sole, whiting, mackerel, shrimps etc. An excellent variety indeed. As are the many ways of preparing seafood, from raw herring to incognito in a range of related products. Fishing as an industry has seen little change over the centuries, as have the shapes of fishing nets. Even today, a fisherman repairing his net manually is not an uncommon sight. It is still a craft;

46 *Fisheries and Shipping*

as is fishing itself. It stands to reason that anyone seriously considering fishing as a career had better get on board at an early age to start looking over the masters' shoulders.

Fisheries and Shipping 47

Dutchmen are Fishermen

Throughout the centuries, shellfish, shrimps, crabs, fish, seals, walruses, whales and, frankly, almost anything else found in the sea, could be served as food. Anything that could not be eaten could be used as tools (e.g. fish hooks), as fuel (whale oil), or even as domestic fencing (whalebones). Moreover, until recently, shells were used to produce shell lime in limekilns. The lime was used in the construction industry as a raw material for building and plastering. Today shells are used as surface material on thousands of kilometres of forest and bicycle paths that criss-cross throughout the Netherlands.

The price of fish is determined by supply and demand, and of course, by the quality. The pricing is based on weight. Fishermen generally have no problem selling their wares, as fish is healthy, tasty and less expensive than meat. Cleaning and smoking fish, eels and herring are tasks best left to the experts.

The Fishing Fyke as been around for 6,000 Years

In ancient times the local population lived off almost anything that was washed up on shore or found in small pools, as well as from whatever they could catch from riverbanks and beaches. Prehistoric man later began to spear fish, sometimes from canoes made from hollowed-out tree trunks, using bone tipped spears with hooks to prevent their prey from escaping. Fishing fykes discovered in Bergschenhoek date back to more than 6,000 years ago. The fykes were made from cornel shoots that were woven together with rush strings. Each fyke was only intended to last one year; however the simplicity of their construction belies the high level of craftsmanship of the manufacturers. Obviously a fyke had to be made well, as the community's survival depended on them, and poorly constructed fykes would yield little or no harvest at all. While materials obviously differed, the ingenious construction techniques used in those ancient fykes, closely resemble those in use today. Fishing on the water, as opposed to angling, became increasingly popular as shipbuilding techniques became more advanced. The old dugouts were systematically replaced by real boats with frame and wood skin constructions. As the centuries passed, the role of shipping, including freight ships, increased enormously; in Roman times flat bottom barges of 34 by 4.5 metres routinely navigated the Rhine.

There is an enormous variety of fishing boats. The boats are well cared for and many small fishing villages have their own shipyards where boats can be taken out of the water for maintenance and repairs. Understandably this is essential to maintain safety on the water.
The fishing village of Bunschoten-Spakenburg still has a substantial 'brown' fishing fleet.

Fisheries and Shipping

The many picturesque towns and cities on the banks of the IJsselmeer date back to the time when local waters were still salty and known as the Zuiderzee (Southern Sea). It is possible to rent a sailing boat in nearly every town – even two-masters. Hoisting a sail means using muscles you never knew you had. A sailing trip is an excellent way to build team spirit and fend off modern stress-related ailments.

Fishing Techniques are Centuries Old

Catches of fish that were not intended for immediate consumption were kept fresh in floating wooden cages until needed. The same technique was used onboard fishing vessels on the Zuiderzee from as early as the late Middle Ages. The ships were constructed with an open centre area (the work space) and double bottom with an open space in between (the fish well) that was linked to the sea via holes on the outside of the ship's hull. In the centre of this space, attached to the floor, was a trough or case that was open at the top and bottom to hold the catch for live delivery to the port. The living quarters were located in the forecastle of the boat. A remarkable fact is that sixty old fishing boats, used as recreational vessels on the IJsselmeer today, are based on the design of those ancient fishing vessels. Old fishermen who worked as ship's boys prior to and immediately after the closure of the Zuiderzee, still worked on those old ships and told tales of how, in the past, herring was so abundant, it was there for the taking. The working

Fisheries and Shipping

week of the fisherman is seven days. The techniques they use today are still based on those used in the Middle Ages. Normally the collective fleets of several small villages would work the ocean together. In the event that they could not make it back to the homeport on Sunday, when no fishing was allowed, the fishermen attended church in the nearest port. This explains the existence of large churches in some of the smallest coastal villages.

Fisheries and Shipping

Thanks to an extensive network of lighthouses, often of peculiar design and striking colour, safe harbours and prominent points along the coast are generally visible from afar. The history of the lighthouse dates back at least 2,200 years; however, it's days may be numbered. Seamen today no longer need the sextant or radio to get an exact fix as it is possible to instantly determine one's exact position by satellite positioning system. Gradually this will make the coded light bundle of the lighthouse redundant.

Gutting, Preserving and Smoking Herring

The entire family, from old to young, used to help to gut, pickle and pack the herring into herring vats. Other techniques, such as smoking, which imbued the fish with an extremely popular aroma, were utilised to preserve the fish for longer periods. The better the smoker knew the art of smoking, the better his fish tasted; so regular competitions were held to identify and reward the best craftsmen. The difficulty of good smoking was almost exactly inversely proportional to the ease of finding the judge and chief taster of the contest. Needless to say, there were always plenty of volunteers for that tasty task. To this day, events such as smoking are popular promotional activities in flourishing Dutch fishing villages.

Fisheries and Shipping

Rowing boats are available for rent along most rivers. In the past, the ferry was the sole means of crossing rivers. The old ferryboats are still around, some even carry cars. However, largely replaced by modern bridges, the ferry is another phenomenon that is fast fading from the Dutch water transportation scene.

Fisheries and Shipping

These days, pleasure boats far outnumber fishing boats. There are jetties everywhere, designed to lure tourists to the festive atmosphere of waterside restaurants and pubs.

54 Nature & Nostalgia

Forgotten and neglected patches of land are some of the most beautiful in the Netherlands – mostly they are found near old estates.

Pages 56 and 57:
Slot Loevestein

Slot Loevestein towers above the surrounding waterscapes. In the evening, its dark silhouette is unmistakable. In days of old this was an ideal bastion of defence against plunderers and hostile armies from neighbouring countries.

Chapter 4

Fortresses, Strongholds, Castles and Pleasure Gardens

Based on general estimates, Holland, over the past few centuries, was graced with no less than some 2,300 castles and nobleman's estates. In the Province of Noord-Holland alone there were 50 to 80, of which only nine castles and ruins remain today. The Betuwe and Overijssel were absolutely littered with castles. Today, no more than 300 remain. There are many reasons for the loss of those ancient monuments. Fortunately, several hundred still remain to grace the Dutch countryside with their pretty gardens and rich plantations. Moreover, both the buildings and their owners played a crucial part in the historical and political development of our country.

The Origin of the Castle

The edifice known as the 'castle' has a long and varied history; but this begs the question as to where it all began. The word, 'castle' is derived from the Roman "castellum", which was nothing more than a small fortified military outpost. Our notion of a castle is a fortified building designed to accommodate the local population. These buildings, known alternately as castles, fortresses, strongholds, manorial farms and 'houses' (in medieval times), had to be fortified because, for many centuries, they were needed to protect inhabitants against attacks from the outside. After all, society was not quite as well organised then as it is today. The first recorded instance of a castle, the so-called "Hunneschans" at Uddel on the Veluwe, dates back to the days of Charlemagne. It was constructed as a surrounding wall and moat with a diameter of approximately one hundred metres, and houses inside – usually a large house for the Saxon lord of the manor and his family, and several smaller hovels for serfs and slaves. Several ruins of larger fortified buildings from later periods, all of which belonged to wealthy chiefs and noblemen, can still be found in Holland today.

These small, fortified communities subsisted entirely on agricultural produce, which explains the nature of the Medieval castle: A central building within a small community of farmers who used the castle for refuge in hazardous times. In most instances, the central building was little more than a defensible farmer's homestead that, in former times, was built of timber. In that situation it is conceivable that one farmer in every community would have proved his mettle as leader, and would have been accepted as such by his community.

From Keep to Castle

The 11th and 12th century version of the castle was known as a motte. The motte was a place of refuge built upon a manmade mound of earth dug out of a surrounding moat. Initially it was built as a wooden bulwark, but later buildings were constructed from stone. The area in the front of the motte, known as the forecourt, was used as a living space for the lord of the manor, and incorporated a farmstead. When danger loomed, the community would retreat into the reinforced stronghold. An original motte, known as the "Burcht", is situated in the centre of Leiden. This structure dates back approximately 1,000 years. In later years the hill was elevated and furnished with a stone bulwark and battlements along the upper front facade. The gantry was probably constructed from timber. Similar buildings can also be found at Kessel in Noord-Limburg and Oostvoorne in Zeeland. These later versions incorporated a number of new features, including a square, stone tower at the centre of the mound, known as a donjon or keep, to accommodate the lord of the manor and his family. This development may well have signalled the advent of the physical separation of the nobleman from his underlings, who continued to live in the forecourt. Moreover, the keep may justifiably be viewed as the origin of the castle. Similar keeps

Professional craftsmen were needed to build castles. In later times, when castles no longer served primarily as fortresses, builders developed a taste for attractive designs.

were also built on flat terrains; in most instances they were solid constructions built on sandy moors or riverbeds with walls of at least two metres thick and cramped quarters. The principal purpose of these massive constructions was to protect the inhabitants against attack. The entrance to the building was on the first floor and could only be reached by means of a ladder. Obviously, this type of castle was extremely primitive, as were the living conditions inside.

Round Castles become Rectangular

Most castles that exist today are rectangular in design; however, the original retreats, with the exception of the discrete towers, were more or less round, as is evident in those at Leiden and Oostvoorne. Another quaint example is Teilingen at Sassenheim. This is a completely round complex, probably from the 12th century, which in contrast to the Burcht in Leiden, has robust living quarters within its walls. Teilingen's fame drives

The moat serves as extra protection around the castle. Soldiers, too, needed protection in the form of a helmet and coat of mail; especially for man-to-man combat. This was however only needed once the castle had already been penetrated - a formidable task, considering the heavy fortification of some castles. Later, in more peaceful times, the courtyard, too, became an area of embellishment.

60   *Fortresses, Strongholds, Castles and Pleasure Gardens*

primarily from Jacoba van Beieren who lived and died within its walls.

The disadvantage of the round fortress was the fact that it served exclusively as a retreat, and the occupants could do little more than await the assailants' next actions. To enable occupants to better defend themselves against their assailants, castle builders later adopted the practise of building towers at strategic points on the wall. Gradually the towers became connected by straight walls, which, in time, yielded the rectangular castle. In most instances those castles were surrounded by a wide moat and were known as a 'moated castle'. It is also believed that, later, diagonal walls were built onto existing keeps, which gradually yielded larger buildings that new owners continued to add to. It is further assumed that Dutch crusaders copied designs from abroad, where most of the enormous, rectangular crusader fortresses were built with massive towers.

Rectangular castles often had forecastles with service buildings and stables. Possibly the best known example of this type is Muiderslot, which is almost completely square, with a tower on every corner. In contrast to most Dutch castles, which were built onto in the course of the centuries, this one appears to be an authentic example of a medieval castle. The castle at Muiderslot was built by Floris V, the Count of Holland, who was the founder of the defensible castle in the Netherlands. He built several, including the almost equally famous grand palace with the renowned Hoghe Sale (Upper Hall) in Den Haag, currently known as the Ridderzaal (Knight's Hall). The original accommodation of this palace is currently still in use.

To this day, the old chatelaine of castle Cannenburch sits, as if turned to stone, on a little garden bench, while, at castle Hoensbroek, we can get a taste of what it must have felt like to be put in the pillory.

Fortresses, Strongholds, Castles and Pleasure Gardens

Artistry reached its finest expression in the ranks of the craftsmen's guilds. Although Amsterdam had no painter's guild, Rembrandt's "The Night Watch" nevertheless became the centrepiece of the Dutch History of Art. This choice is hardly strange in view of the countless wars and disputes throughout the ages – standing guard, whether by day or night, could, in most instances, make the difference between life and death.

The Feudal System arose for Practical Reasons

It is quite clear that castle-building techniques evolved in time. This phenomenon had everything to do with social developments, particularly with relationships of power. In the Middle Ages, Holland was far from the all-inclusive sovereign state it is today. The country consisted of many counties and duchies, such as Gelre, Brabant, Holland, and smaller ones, such as Kessel and Horne in Limburg, and Bronckhorst in Gelderland. However, many of the ruling counts were not really wealthy enough to maintain an appropriate state, administrate large counties and fight the necessary battles for their counties. Instead, the landlords granted local noblemen sections of land on loan, which entitled the noblemen to a

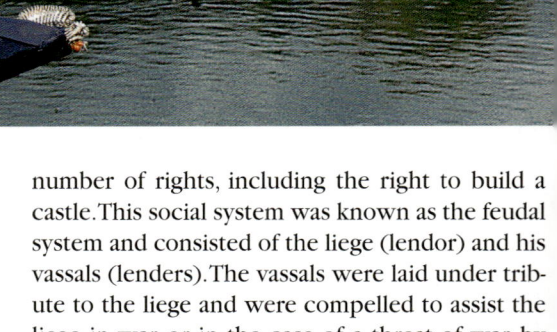

number of rights, including the right to build a castle. This social system was known as the feudal system and consisted of the liege (lendor) and his vassals (lenders). The vassals were laid under tribute to the liege and were compelled to assist the liege in war, or in the case of a threat of war, by providing soldiers. The counts, for their part, were vassals to the German king or Emperor.

The liege was himself entitled to a host of highly gratifying rights, such as the 'One Tenth Right' (tiendenrecht), which entitled him to one tenth of the complete harvests of all his vassals, and the

62 *Fortresses, Strongholds, Castles and Pleasure Gardens*

so-called "tinzenrecht", which, among other things, entitled the liege to a percentage of his vassals' poultry. His powers further included the execution of law, administration and legislation in his region. In some instances he was entitled to impose tollage and ferry levies, as well as the sole right to own swans and pigeons; which explains the beautiful pigeon cotes found on some estates. In addition, he had sole hunting rights and exclusive "Rights to the Wind", which entailed that farmers in his domain were compelled to use his mills to produce flour from their grain.

In the Middle Ages, castle dwellers kept flocks of geese around their fortresses. They may have enjoyed roast goose on the odd occasion, but this practise was primarily aimed at alerting the inhabitants to the presence of approaching strangers by day and night. Geese tend to stir up an infernal row in the presence of friend and foe.

Fortresses, Strongholds, Castles and Pleasure Gardens

Many Battles Fought

The sweet taste of so power over others must have tempted these landlords to go even further. On the other hand, many vassals soon forgot that it was to their lieges that they owed their privileged positions, and like minor royalties, their greed soon compelled them to endeavour to expand their domains. Naturally, it was possible to do so by peaceable means, such as a marriage of convenience, receiving an inheritance, or by purchasing more land. But it was also possible to expand, or lose, your realm of power by the sword. Many vassals changed their loyalty from one liege to another; for example, from the Count of Gelre to the Count of Holland or vice versa. Needless to say, this frequently resulted in battle. On the other hand, 'battle' is perhaps too big a word; a typical military occupation of a castle consisted of an average army of twenty-five soldiers. For example, for the siege of Polanen castle

Once cannons became sufficiently powerful to pulverise castle walls, the practise of building reinforced castles was abandoned, and builders began to build stronger fortresses. Existing cities were also converted into fortified cities. Battles were executed in the open fields.

64 *Fortresses, Strongholds, Castles and Pleasure Gardens*

(it no longer exists), in 1351, William V, the Count of Holland had an army of only 26 men and 24 English archers, who had been imported for the occasion. Not exactly a spectacular army to conduct an historical siege. The castle was taken by means of the battering ram - an important weapon of war in those days.

There were other weapons too, of course; such as the catapult, which was used to hurl stones into the besieged castle. Sometimes it was used to hurl contaminated animal carcasses into the occupied castle, inducing the starving rank and file to succumb to a host of horrific diseases. Another useful weapon of assault was a wooden tower that could be raised to the level of the castle wall, and moved to the wall to allow the attackers access to the battlements via an extendible gangway after which the battle could continue man to man.

In later centuries those battles were conducted in neat uniforms whereby tight lines of fusiliers would exchange fire until the time came to charge the enemy with the bayonet – a practise that, among other things, devastated many a tidy uniform.

Fortresses, Strongholds, Castles and Pleasure Gardens

The Castle Lost it Purpose

Horrific as those stories were, they add a certain romance to our vision of the Middle Ages. The advent of the cannon, in the fourteenth century, changed everything. Man had invented gunpowder, or had adopted it from the Chinese. After that, no castle could offer a truly safe retreat. The very concept of the castle became less meaningful. There were other reasons too for the gradual decline of nobility and their little domains. One such reason was the booming phenomenon of the city.

Moreover, as Holland was absorbed, first by Burgundy and later by the Hapsburg Empire, the world itself seemed to expand. The petty battle for the little patch of earth became a thing of the past. At the same time, war continued to scorch the earth on a larger scale, and the technology of war continued to improve. As the cannon began to dominate the battlefield, sovereigns began to build fortresses, such as those at Naarden and Bourtange, and Heusden in the vicinity of Den

In the 16th century, the scope of the sovereign state expanded and they were less easily conquered. As a result, sovereigns and stadholders (viceroys) could afford to build beautiful unfortified palaces without

66 *Fortresses, Strongholds, Castles and Pleasure Gardens*

Bosch. Heusden is an interesting example of a simple medieval keep that, through many extensions in the Middle Ages evolved into a castle and later, from the 15th century on, into a highly reinforced fortress.

For castle owners, however, the constant threat of attack systematically faded. As the evil of war subsided, so did the landlord and his subjects' need for the protection of the castle. A time finally dawned when it was almost possible to live an enjoyable life; which is exactly what happened. In the harsh life of the Middle Ages, the castle was little more than a cold retreat, especially for the lower nobility with limited means. Most castles consisted of a residential tower, with the donjon or keep, a dungeon for provisions, a living room and a sleeping area above. Privacy was an alien concept in those days, as man and wife shared sleeping quarters with all and sundry – there was simply no space to indulge in 'common decency'.

the constant threat of destruction. The lower nobility, too, could afford to preside over larger estates with a greater sense of pomp. A favourite pastime was to be driven around the estate in a finely embellished coach drawn by a team of immaculately groomed horses. In times of relative peace, they built ornamental gardens around the manor, and only the landlord was entitled to hunt on his own estate.

Fortresses, Strongholds, Castles and Pleasure Gardens

More than 60 species of mammals can be found in our country; most of which are protected today. Hunting is limited to a few specific species, and the kill continues to be the ultimate aim of the hunt. This tradition has however been changed in contemporary drag hunting - today's hunters call their tallyhos behind packs of raving dogs hot on the trail of a rag dipped in fox urine. This acceptable practise seems to appease the hunting instinct in most contemporary hunters – no animals are killed and a jolly good time is had by all. Horn blowers accompany the motley hunts with piercing calls summoned from their horns.

Fortresses, Strongholds, Castles and Pleasure Gardens

The Castle as Pleasure Resort

From the 16th century, the castle became a resort – a haven for the pursuit of the good life. While, in the past, only the wealthier lords were able to decorate their castles with flair, the lower nobility also began to enjoy those privileges. Decorative touches included glass panes in windows, fancy furniture, wall dressings and silverware. The nobility occupying these latter day homes made it a point of honour to live up to their illustrious family names; and their homes became pleasure resorts.

Houses were remodelled to the latest styles, gardens designed and hunting parties organised in local pastures and surrounding forests. After the Eighty Year War, the Netherlands became a comfortable little republic, run by aldermen who enjoyed the luxuries of castles (Frederik Hendrik), and palaces (William III, Palace Het Loo), many of which did not survive the ravages of time.

Moreover, at this time a new class of builder of country estates entered the market – the wealthy merchants. The elegant country houses built by

Healthy forests play host to a great variety of fungi, moulds and beetle larvae that naturally clear the forests of fallen wood and other types of debris. Hedgehogs chase beetles in the thickets, while the shy pheasant scratches about the forest floor for fallen seeds. The pheasant is not indigenous to the Netherlands, and was specifically imported for the hunter's benefit. In spite of man's tendency to leave his mark wherever he passes, nature has always coped better without man's ambitious intrusion.

the citizens of Amsterdam on the banks of the River Vecht are distinguishable from Middle Age castles by their symmetric designs. Many of these stately homes have since been lost. Which takes us back to the beginning of our story: Many castles and graceful country houses were lost in wars and floods, and due to financial failure, demolition and a general sense of apathy. Today the interest has returned, and those stately edifices that remain are well appreciated; which is something we should be grateful for.

Pages 70 and 71:
The forest is perhaps most beautiful in autumn, with its red and golden light and gently falling leaves.

On occasion, one becomes aware of the chainsaw roaring elsewhere in the forest. Where mighty trees fall, cup lichen soon moves in to occupy the remaining trunks.

Nature & Nostalgia

Porcelain fungi derive their names from their shining glazed caps. Forestry officials consciously leave the trunks behind to encourage the growth of mushrooms and insects, which, in turn, attract other hungry denizens of the forest. In this way, they hope to blow life back into our forests.

Nature & Nostalgia

On tourist fishing days the ladies from the fishing villages simply continue their daily toil. They are usually happy to explain their elaborate handicrafts to curious tourists. In the evenings, they are quite as capable of preparing a tasty mush from grandma's days.

74   Nature & Nostalgia

Chapter 5

Crafts

The true craftsman is a member of a dying breed. That not withstanding, there are still quite a few excellent craftsmen that are capable of reproducing products that have been around for thousands of years. Some continue to work with raw materials that were used long before the year of our Lord. The tailor is one such example. Today, while extremely costly, it is possible to hire a tailor to produce a suit of clothing. From prehistoric times to well after the Industrial Revolution all clothing was tailor-made. Wool-weaving techniques are ancient, as is the art of pottery making. In our day and age pottery making has been elevated to the level of the arts. However, in the south of Holland, in the Neolithic Age, some 6,000 years ago, robust earthenware beakers, known as Bandkeramiks, were produced for daily use. Although not shaped on the potter's wheel, but by hand, our ancient ancestors did use clay, which is the same raw material used today. Prehistoric craftsmen also used raw materials such as leather. Archaeologists discovered complete leather shoes dating back approximately 4,000 in the peat bogs of the province of Drenthe. Most shoes today are factory made; yet the shoemaker is still around to repair them.

Bronze and iron were also used to produce tools and weapons long before the year of our Lord. Which brings us to a craftsman that is truly as old as the world – the blacksmith. While his may be a dying craft, there are still quite a few around. Prehistoric man cast smelted bronze into moulds to create objects, such as axes. Today, the art of casting bronze is more or less limited to the domain of the sculptor.

Craftsmen are Artists

Craftsmen are individuals that are skilled in producing utensils by hand. While this may appear to be a reasonable definition, it might be added that they generally do so on demand. In other words, they produce their wares at other people's request. However, in the past this type of craftsman could only be found in the larger communities, such as in the cities - not on farms, and certainly not in prehistoric times.

The celt, a handy utensil that was produced in prehistoric times, may well have been the first utensil made by craftsmen. It certainly demanded the necessary manual skills. However, those early craftsmen, who were mostly members of communities no larger than a one-family unit, undoubtedly made their tools for their own private use. The same applies to the stone arrowheads and hooked bone spearheads used by prehistoric hunters and fishermen.

What is it that really sets art and the crafts apart? Were the stonecutters of the first centuries AD that created the exquisite sculpted altars dedicated to Nehallenia, the goddess of fishermen, artists or mere craftsmen? The altars were fished out of the Oosterschelde, in a sanctuary that was dry land at the time. And what was the artistic status of the stonemasons who were responsible for the construction of some of the most beautiful churches on Earth? Although they created truly beautiful objects, they were probably mere craftsmen working to the design of an artistic designer. The makers of exquisite knights' suits of armour in the 14th and 15th century were likewise considered craftsmen. As were the cabinetmakers (a craft that still flourishes today) that created cabinets with inlays and carvings of superior artistic quality. Were they artists, or mere craftsmen? Who really knows?

The Dutch take pride in producing traditional handicrafts, such as jams and other foodstuffs. Traditional painting belies a steady hand and solid patience, while plaiting entails profound knowledge of materials and technique.

The Romans Brought New Crafts

There are many authentic handicrafts around today. Some, such as bread baking, basket weaving, metal forging, felt making, dyeing, spinning, weaving, bone work, leather tanning, and pottery making, date back to prehistoric times. Many others, including mintage and glass blowing in the form of drinking glasses and bottles, have survived through Roman times. While glass, as such, is older, the first records of glass blowing date back to approximately the year of our Lord. The Romans introduced a host of new handicrafts to the Lowlands, including construction techniques, such as roof tile manufacturing, and the production of pipelines for baths and so on. Skilled technicians or craftsmen with kilns were needed to produce these items. The baked brick was another Roman invention. Our own craftsmen built wood and loam houses with thatched roofs – a building technique, which, in spite of the existence of the brick, continues to be used to this day. Many houses built by skilled craftsmen can still be viewed in the province of Zuid-Limburg. Some handicrafts that have been around since the dawn of man, flourished during the Middle Ages; this includes the manufacture of a number of utensils, such as combs that were made from bone and animal horn. Candlestick makers made candles from beeswax and sheep's fat, and fishermen made their own fishing nets. The cabinet-maker made chests, tables and wall shelves for pots, pans and crockery, while the shoemaker used cow, calf and goat hide to make shoes, and the cooper made buckets and jugs, and vats to hold wine, beer and meat. The barber was an extraordinary craftsman who not only trimmed beards, but also doubled as surgeon to treat injuries.

True craftsmen are hard to find today, and a wealth of knowledge has been lost due to the fact that almost anything can be made cheaper by machine. Craftsmanship has largely been relegated to the status of creative pastime, or as a source of extra income practised on weekends. One craft that is still very much alive today is the art of the farrier; after all, horses, although they have evolved from beast of burden to draught animal to domestic animal, used mainly for sports and recreational purposes today, still need old-fashioned professional hoof care.

People who are inspired by the past often endeavour to keep the craft alive by rediscovering forgotten knowledge. This is often done in groups or associations. They endeavour to turn back the hands of time by, for example, reproducing objects dating back to the Middle Ages as authentically as possible. They produce and wear clothing, shoes, and jewellery from former times. They also reproduce authentic tools and use them to, e.g. produce and eat foods that were typical in ancient times. Enthusiasts would, for instance, permit only the use of an authentic hand drill (albeit reconstructed) to create a tool from deer bone. Needless to say, these nostalgic enthusiasts remain at all times informed of the latest archaeological discoveries that may help them unravel the tantalising puzzles of history.

Crafts 77

Then came the Specialist and then the Shop!

There was an important difference between the rural areas, the small agricultural communities, and the burgeoning phenomenon of the city. The farming family did everything for their own use; baking, butchering, pickling meat, spinning, weaving and building. In the rural community one man could do everything, whereas in the fast-growing cities, labour division soon became a reality. In the cities, craftsmen increasingly began to specialise in a single craft. Moreover, skilled artisans began to make a living by manufacturing products for others. In short, the dawning of the age of specialisation was upon us - a phenomenon that would become consolidated over the hundreds of years that followed. City dwellers no longer made their own utensils and foodstuffs, but bought them elsewhere. Generally, in the early days, consumers would buy their products from the craftsman's shop adjacent to his workshop. Thus began a whole new line of industry - the shop owner and trader.

There are many steps between the shearing of the sheep and the final woollen sweater, cap or robe. Shearing is an art in itself; especially if the sheep has ideas of its own. The spinning wheel was a giant leap forward in man's development, but is nevertheless an extremely time-consuming labour. Then there is dyeing and weaving; whether in traditional patterns or creative designs, or a surprising crocheted coat protector on the back of a typical Dutch "grandma's bicycle".

Food, Clothes and a House

The main handicrafts were based on man's primary needs – sustenance, clothing and shelter. In other words, foodstuff production, textiles and the construction industry were the fundamental trades. Undoubtedly, much of the food sold in the cities was imported from outside the city walls; however, the most basic foodstuff, throughout the ages, namely bread, always came from the baker. Bakers have been around since the 12th century. Human beings also need to consume liquids. Because the water in local rivers and moats was mostly filthy, man invented the inspired art of brewing. Because, in those days, most foods were pickled, ancient city dwellers understandably developed enormous thirsts; which partially explains the enormous quantities of beer consumed. By the year 1500, the city of Haarlem had around 120 breweries. Gouda and Delft probably had no fewer. Naturally these breweries were small boutique affairs, and not the mass production facilities we know today.

Since time immemorial, sheep provided the raw materials for man's clothing – wool. It was only much later that our ancestors began to develop the techniques required to produce linen from flax. The textile industry was an essential component of the industrial development of many Dutch cities, and Leiden was without a doubt the industry leader. An old textile building known as the 'Lakenhal' ('Cloth Hall') has been preserved in Leiden. The name is somewhat confusing, as it refers to the end product – woollen cloth. Leiden enjoyed two boom cycles in the history of the textile industry. During the second boom period, around 1610, Leiden was the undisputed leading textile centre in Europe. The wool was originally imported from England, but later also from Spain. Delivery from Spain continued throughout the Eighty Year War, but in the form of a lighter and cheaper type of textile. Haarlem, on the other hand, was the linen capital of Holland. Linen production demanded crystal clear water, which had to be pumped from the local dunes. While textile manufacturing in Leiden was an industry in itself, the various types of treatment, such as pulling and plucking, combing, spinning, weaving, raising and pressing also constituted specialised trades.

Crafts 79

Who's bidding…?! 10, 20, 50, 80, 125 guilders…..no further bids? Once, twice, three times, sold! To the gentleman with the Zeeland cap! Rich farmers enjoyed flaunting their material worth with Delft Blue crockery in their display cabinets – Delft porcelain was once an indispensable status symbol. Sadly, in leaner years, proud owners were sometimes forced to sell part of their collections to ensure survival.

82   Crafts

Fresh mussels from Zeeland are a delicacy that can be prepared in many different ways. The true connoisseur eats mussels raw from the shell – bon appetite!

The Guilds: High Quality at Appointed Prices

The oldest known guilds are the merchant's guilds, one of the oldest being a guild established in the merchant city of Tiel in 1018. Small craftsmen formed the core of most of the ancient guilds. The Master Craftsman, who was a member of the guild of his chosen profession, usually had one or more apprentices working for him. Normally, after seven years an apprentice would be promoted to the rank of journeyman. Upon completion of the master's examination (if successful) and payment of a substantial admission fee, the journeyman would become a Master Craftsman.

The two principal objectives of the guilds were to guarantee high quality levels, and to suppress competition. The guilds were characterised by an extremely rigid regime - everything was prescribed; from the number of students per master, the time dedicated to the production of a product and the type of tools to use, to wages, and, of course, prices. Non-members caught practising a trade (moonlighters or fly-by-nights), could look forward to a hefty term in prison. This rigid, monopolistic structure finally led to the dissolution of the guild system. The trade guilds were important institutions from approximately the 13th century to 1798, when they were abolished by decree – the event that heralded the age of free enterprise.

Social and cultural institutions represented another face of the guild system. Sick and invalid guild members, and their widows, were entitled to financial support, and the strong sense of social cohesion was expressed in festive banquets where members passed around the silver guild cup (on display in many museums). The guild was also represented in the church, where the patron saint of every guild had its own altar; e.g. Saint Eloy or Eligius in the case of the gold and silver smiths. While the guilds are a thing of the past, in the Netherlands, the rifle clubs are still known as 'Shooter's Guilds.

Crafts

The Oldest Windmills are Medieval

The post-mill is most probably the oldest type of mill there is – it has been around since the 12th century. An illustration exists of a later version in Flanders in approximately 1280, which, while primitive, is very recognisable. In fact, the 46 post-mills in the Netherlands (all built later), especially those in Gelderland, Noord-Brabant and Limburg, are very similar to the older machine in Flanders. It is also fascinating to realise that the post-mill, which was the medieval workhorse supreme, never really changed over the centuries. In fact, this is true for all windmills, including later models, such as the smockmills, which also date back to around 1430. While the smockmill resembles the post-mill in appearance, flour production occurred at ground level rather than in the upper section. None of these industrial-strength smockmills exist today. Our smockmills are smaller versions that were used to displace excess water by means of a diagonal jackscrew with screw thread, protected by a sheath, that moved the water to a ditch or canal at higher elevation during rotation. The jackscrew was driven by a system of rotating vanes, axes, a vertical central main piece or king post, and a transmission gear system.

Most of the 70 smockmills still in existence today (the oldest mills in Holland) displace water by means of a large vertical waterwheel, similar to the two-thousand year old watermills in the east of the country.

Holland is sometimes called the Land of the Frogs. Certainly there are plenty of frogs here! Why? Abundant water, of course. For centuries the Dutch have been struggling to contain the water surrounding them. In the early days this was done with windmills, which worked rather effectively, as the

country is also exposed to a great deal of wind. The windmills were used to dry and keep the polders dry, and to reclaim large inland lakes – a process known as impoldering. To do so, many windmills were built in long rows along newly constructed dikes. The Kinderdijk is an impressive example of such a row of windmills. They have been a source of inspiration for many an artist; an activity that the miller and his family had little or no time for in their busy days. Scrubbing the washing, for instance, and leaving it out in the sun to dry or bleach beside the mill and pastures surrounding it.

Windmills   89

The Mill as Forerunner of Modern Mechanics

Smock watermills are small, as is their operational capacity. The later, more common models with thatched hoods found predominantly in the west of the Netherlands are somewhat larger. However, before elaborating on those, I would like to introduce another old faithful, the tower mill. The tower mill is the oldest mill in the Netherlands and, of the original 27, only four have survived the ravages of time. Undoubtedly the fact that they were built from brick has something to do with this. The mills are located in Zevenaar and Zeddam, and were built around 1450. The tower mill is a very straight, heavy brick tower with a rotating hood on top. This is a very simple construction to operate, because, unlike the post-mill, where the miller had to turn the entire construction to face the wind, here only the hood needs to be turned.

The turning mechanism is located inside the hood, and these windmills are known in Dutch as a "bovenkruier" or a top-turner. The slightly diagonal upper axis turned inside the hood and was connected to the vane. The upper wheel was fitted around the upper axis in the hood and was fitted with short wooden pins known as the cams. The cams could be compared to the cogs of a gearwheel. This system was designed to grip into the cams or the mutually separate bars of a vertically turning wheel (known in Dutch as the "bovenbonkelaar"), which is attached to the central main piece. From a technical perspective, all mills are simply mechanical systems of rotating wooden axes and cogwheels. The ultimate purpose of all wheat mills, such as the tower mills, is to drive the upper millstone (known as the 'runner') via an ingenious transmission system. The bottom millstone is known as the 'sleeper'. Both stones have an outward fanning grooved profile that conducts the flour out of the stones and into the flour bags. The grain is fed in via the centre of the runner. In the near perfect 17th century wheat mills, the input level of the wheat could be adjusted to the strength of the wind.

Windmill maintenance is a never-ending task; it is labour intensive and extremely costly. There are few monuments that are so directly affected by wind and weather as the windmill. To stay in sound working condition, the multitude of wooden turning parts and thatch roofing need to be replaced regularly by experts. Obviously the thatchers and carpenters need to be seasoned experts.

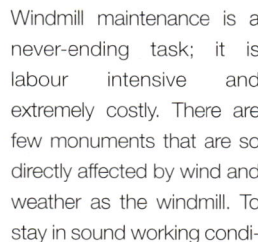

Windmills

The miller earns a bit of extra cash for mill maintenance through his little shop or by charging enthusiastic visitors on open days or upon request. Visitors today can buy pancake and bread flour for home baking (a practise which is gaining popularity), as well as various other types and mixes of flour from a number of mills. On the remaining days of the week, the miller uses the mill for production purposes; from sawing timber to milling grain. The preservation of the mills has made it possible for visitors to gain insight into an ancient technology. The operation of the millstone, tackle and capstan wheel is the exclusive duty of the fully qualified miller.

Pages 92 and 93:
Holland

Schiedam has the Largest Mill in the World

More recent windmill designs were not only better designed, but also taller to allow access to wind above high city buildings. The later tower mills were tall stone or brick structures with galleries positioned halfway up on the outside of the mill where the turning mechanism was located. That explains why these mills were also known as 'upper-outside turners' (boven-buitenkruier). The mills had a tail that extended downwards from the hood. The tail was designed in the form of a number of beams that converged at the turning wheel. The turning wheel was a spoke wheel attached to an axis around which chains were wound, so that the wheel could be fastened to various points on the tower. By turning the wheel, the miller could turn the mill to face the wind.

The height of the tower mills provided several advantages; in addition to catching more wind, they offered a substantial amount of storage space. The base contained a door that was large enough to allow a wagon to enter and deliver raw materials. These industrial mills were designed to grind almost any type of raw material, including flour, paints, spices, oils and malt - the latter for Dutch gin distilleries in Schiedam, where a number of these mills can still be seen today. In fact, Schiedam is the home of the tallest windmill in the world. Most mills were 'baptised', and the giant at Schiedam, which measures almost 45 metres to the tips of its vanes, is known as 'De Noord' (The North).

Although there is probably no other place in the Netherlands with quite as many industrial mills as the Zaanstreek, there are still quite a few around. For example, there are five working mills at Zaanse Schans in Zaandam that are still used to process oil, paint, paper, timber and grains. The latter is used primarily for barley hulling – barley being the raw material for pearl barley. Barley porridge was a staple food in Holland in the olden days. The timber mill, a type of post-mill, is an almost square design with a widening body towards the base, and building extensions to the left and right. The entire building is turned at the base to face the wind. These post-mills first appeared in Holland around 1600, and were used in the Zaanstreek to cut planks from timber imported from Scandinavia. The planks were used for housing and in ship construction, which was

a flourishing industry in that area at the time. Czar Peter the Great, for one, came to this region to study local shipbuilding techniques. The Dutch term for this type of mill, the 'paltrokmolen', was borrowed from the name of the short, 15th- and 16th-century men's coat that widened out to the bottom and was known locally as a 'paltrok'.

Polder Mills made Holland what it is

Although there are various types of mills in the Netherlands, the best known is, undoubtedly, the polder mill, a wind-water mill dating back to 1407, which I have photographed on many occasions. These lightweight all-wood octagonal mills were designed to stand on soggy earth, and were covered with a hood of thatch. The mills displaced water by means of a wooden paddle wheel or jackscrew and it would be fair to say that the west of our country and Friesland would not have been the same today without these mills.

The lowlands of the Netherlands are ideal for exploring by bicycle. The country is criss-crossed with special bicycle paths and neat asphalt farm roads. However, it is much more romantic to explore the countryside along the seemingly endless network of waterways. A good map and a little planning will take the traveller past many mills, ancient farmsteads and nature reserves. To keep the waterways navigable, they need to be dredged on a regular basis. Although this is a noisy activity, it is essential to prevent the waterways from silting up. Ear mufflers provide essential relief.

The principle purpose of these mills was to dry swampy land for livestock and crop cultivation, as well as to reclaim land from numerous inland lakes. The Schermer Lake in the province of Noord-Holland was dried around 1630. Once the dike had been built around the lake, some 51 mills were used to pump the area dry over a period of 4 years. Collectively their paddle wheels moved some 1,000 m? of water per minute. The brain behind this project was Jan Adriaansz Leeghwater (his last name literally means "Empty water"!).

There are 65 of these polder mills in existence today. The mills were called 'inside turners', which refers to the fact that the miller had to climb to the hood and use a turning wheel to turn the mill to face the wind. Most of the mills in the province of Zuid-Holland are 'outside turners', i.e. the turning wheel was installed on the ground floor - a less cumbersome arrangement for the miller. The mills are also known as 'ground sailors', because the miller could fasten vane sails from the ground in low wind conditions.

Undoubtedly the best known windmills in the Netherlands today is the group located at Kinderdijk. The group of 19 mills have been declared international cultural monuments. Obviously these, and other Dutch windmills, are well worth preserving as national monuments. There are several Dutch organisations dedicated to the upkeep and preservation of the local mills, including a Miller's Guild (again!), an association and several foundations. We owe our gratitude to these organisations for helping to maintain Holland's image as the land of the windmill.

Nature & Nostalgia

Pages 98 and 99:
These black and white Frisian cows inquisitively approach a passer-by at the gate.

The Dutch live on a river delta and the coast, in a land they fashioned in the course of an ongoing battle against water. Perhaps this struggle contributed to the practical nature of the Hollanders, who are known to be rather direct in their social interactions. When a Dutch person says something, he or she usually means it. In other words, Dutch people do not like to beat about the bush. Perhaps their struggle against water has made the Dutch rather less philosophical as a nation – there was no time to philosophise - they became a nation of doers, entrepreneurs, traders, shipbuilders; making the most of the sea in their backyard. On land they make sober, self-reliant farmers. But none of this necessarily means that the Dutch are a boring people; they love their cup of coffee as much as the next man, and will rarely pass up on a pint of beer. They are creative souls too, as demonstrated by their traditional costumes, which differ from region, and from town to town. They have always showed exceptional creativity in their interaction with the land - there are few countries in the world with such a high agricultural production yield as the Netherlands.

100 *Nature & Nostalgia*

Part II ...and the Hollanders

A Farmstead is an Industrial Building

The ancient wooden frame construction has actually never really changed. All farmsteads, whether they were built in 1400 or in 1750, in the Betuwe, Noord-Holland or in the province of Overijssel, began with supporting frame constructions rather than walls, which were only finished off afterwards. Obviously, the technique was refined in later years, but essentially it survived as used by our agricultural ancestors of the Bronze Age. Personally, I find the continuity astounding. The couple trusses of the later farmsteads were built by carpenters in their workshops and conveyed to the construction site in sections. In fact, it is the blueprint for the 'prefab' homes of today.

The design of these structures also determined the interior layout of the buildings. The space inside and above the couple trusses was known as the nave, and the lower outer spaces under the slanting roof were known as the side aisles - precisely the same names used in church buildings. These spaces accommodated all of the indoor facets of the farmer's professional and domestic life, with the former most probably playing the principal role in those early days. By far the greatest part of the farmstead was used to house livestock, store hay, and the harvest and, from the beginning of the 20th century, agricultural equipment. In short, a farmstead was really an industrial building, which was also used for living in.

Although there is an incredible variety of farmsteads in the Netherlands, most of them share the following common features; the cow stall, storage space for hay and/or grain (the pile), a threshing floor, and home. In addition, some farmsteads also accommodate horses' stables. In most cases, all those spaces are accommodated under a single roof - mostly with the home in front, the stalls under one of the side aisles, and the pile in the centre, at the back or at the top of the nave. Of course, hay always was, and continues to be, kept in haystacks.

The Natural Environment Determines the Type of Agriculture

The variations in farmstead layout and design are primarily determined by natural circumstances. Farmers in the province of Zuid-Holland definitely live under different environmental conditions from those in the province of Twente. The principal requirements of the former were a large cow stall and extensive storage space for fodder. In addition, as they produced cheese and butter to sell on the property, they needed space to produce those dairy products, as well as a dedicated area where milk and cream could be separated. The soil in Twente was significantly less fertile and farmers practised mixed farming, e.g.; cattle had to be provided with supplementary fodder, which influenced the construction of the stalls.

Farms were already quite comfortable in the Bronze Age, between 3,700 and 1,300 years ago (the similarities with a modern sheep fold are striking). Part of the house was

104 *Farms and Traditional Costumes*

The house was constructed as a deep litter, or type of pit so that cow droppings could routinely be covered over with peat. As a result, the floor of the stall grew gradually higher and had to be emptied at a certain point. The contents were sprinkled across the barren soil to complete a natural recycling process.

In the early days in Twente, farmers also built so-called 'loose houses' ('los huus') - long buildings in which man and animal lived under the same roof. Moreover, the inhabitants also cooked on an open fire, which was intended to keep the entire homestead warm. The fireplace was not connected to a chimney, so the smoke dissipated through openings in the roof. While this was not especially convenient, the warm smoke served the useful purpose of preserving grains that were stored upstairs in the nave. These 'primordial' farmsteads served local farmers admirably until the beginning of the 20th century.

Four Main Types of Farmsteads

The average farmhouse was somewhat more comfortable, especially in farms located on fertile soil, which yielded greater wealth than sandy soils. Farmsteads in the Netherlands are divided into four general types. The Frisian group in Noord-Holland, those above the River IJ, the in Friesland and Groningen houses, and the hall-house in the remaining provinces except Zeeland and Zuid-Limburg. The unique Zeeland design is particularly remarkable as the family home was built separate from the farmstead. The southern group in Limburg has a foreign appearance to most Dutch people.

Authentic Limburg farmsteads deviate substantially from the rest of the country; for example, the work and living areas are built in a square design around an inner courtyard. While these buildings sometimes appear cut off from the outside world, they can also be aesthetically very impressive. Moreover, as they do not have the standard low slanting roof, they also do not have a nave/aisle construction. With the exception of a few craftsmen's style homes (not unique to Limburg), most of these homesteads, even the oldest ones, are built with brick and mortar. Most craftsmen's houses are wooden frame constructions in which the walls in the spaces between the support beams are covered with sticks and woven wooden slats that are plastered with loam. Loam is one of the best types of insulation available, and completely natural. In most of the other parts of the country brick houses have been the standard for a long time.

designed for eating, living and sleeping, while the rest was reserved for livestock. The front door consisted of a frame of woven willow branches covered with animal hide to keep out the worst cold. In the Bronze Age, the farmer's wife baked bread in clay ovens in homemade clay pots, and the livestock roamed freely about the yard.

Farmers on the West Frisian Islands had a hard life, but converted all flotsam on the beaches into valuable resources. They were known as beachcombers, and there are still quite a few of those around today. The hard life of the beachcombers were immortalised in the novel "Sil, the Beachcomber" ("Sil de strandjutter"). The book was filmed on a typical Terschelling farm, as shown in the photograph above. Sadly, many of the nostalgic tools from the 'good old days' are being lost in contemporary agricultural practise, for example, leaking milk cans

under thatch awnings, haystacks, traditional costumes, elaborate, but stylish barns and quaint but robust mailboxes on street corners in small towns. Even the genetic makeup of the sheep is currently subject to change!

The Extreme Variation is Fascinating

There are around thirty subdivisions within this general breakdown of farmstead designs. The typical Frisian farmstead is the high, square cloche-shaped house found in Noord-Holland, where the work and home areas are built around the central hay storage area. A Frisian variation of this design is called the 'kop-hals-rompboerderij' or 'head-neck-torso farmstead', and the renowned Oldampster farmsteads in Groningen with their impressive manors located at the front. The hall houses found in the rest of the country come in many shapes and sizes. There are the 'achterbaanders' in North-west Drenthe, the 'keuterboerderijtjes' on the sand flats of the Veluwe, the wide, low farmsteads in the Gooi area, the cosy T-shaped farmhouses in the river regions, the long-walled farmsteads of Noord-Brabant and the houses with their enormous Flemish barns in the west of the province. In addition, there are the many local varieties. For those with an interest in old rural buildings, a tour of Dutch farmsteads can yield a fascinating and nostalgic adventure.

Farms and Traditional Costumes

Daily milk production of cow is continuously being increased. As a result, pastures now only have a single type of grass based on high dairy yields. There is no space left for flowers and herbs - a direct cause of the fertilizer problem and the high incidence of ammonium levels in nature. The dunghills of former years were not a bad idea, because pure manure was very popular with crop cultivators.

Farms and Traditional Costumes

Costumes are also Regional Traditions

As in the case of farmsteads, traditional costumes in rural and fishing villages also have a strong regional character. The purpose of the uniformity of dress was to promote a sense of belonging in the community, and to distinguish the wearer from inhabitants of other towns and regions. Unfortunately, this colourful tradition has all but died out, and traditional costumes can almost exclusively be seen at folkloristic events. All that not withstanding, the tradition is very old; for example, the costumes in Gelderland and the Overijssel are of Saxon origins, while the metal headdresses worn by women (reminiscent of modern earphones) derive from Old Germanic traditions. The headdresses are covered by a bonnet, and are sometimes used to attach decorations, such as the rectangular golden plates worn in Zeeland and known as 'stikken'. In Staphorst, the headdress sports a silver curl from under a black silken bonnet. Costumes were also common in medieval cities; however, under pressure of fashion trends, that custom gradually faded in the 17th century. In the rural areas, however, traditional costumes survived for several centuries more.

Cosiness was key to domestic bliss in tiny village homes (and still is), and a cup of coffee was always welcome. For better or for worse, due to the proximity of the neighbours, small town communities exert a high level of social control on their community. One of the benefits was neighbourly help. To demonstrate their solidarity, villagers used to wear identical costumes. Moreover, every town in every region had its own identifying characteristics. For special events and festivities they customarily added detailed embellishments to their costumes. Goats generally could not care less either way - as long as there was plenty to eat.

The Farmers Wife was more Colourful than her Husband

While there were many regional differences, the differences within a given community were always functional. Children had their own costumes, as did married and unmarried men and women, and widows and widowers, all of whom were recognisable by their distinctive costumes. On the whole, women's clothing was more colourful than men's black trousers and coats, which were often embellished with large silver buttons. In the course of time, the costume of the farmer's wife also became less colourful. The colours used most frequently were (dark) red, (dark) green and (dark) blue. From the 17th century, it was customary to imprint cotton fabrics with floral and animal prints. This trend was followed by the advent of colourful, chequered gingham.

There are still many old farmsteads in Holland today. This is mainly due to the fact that not every nook and cranny of the land needs to be used for agricultural purposes. Today, some farmyards are covered in seasonal flowers. Flowers today are an important commercial produce; whether grown on an experimental flower farm or simply for show, it's beautiful to behold.

Farms and Traditional Costumes 111

Two Familiar Examples: Staphorst and Zuid-Beveland

The traditional costumes of Staphorst and Zeeland are reasonably well known. In Staphorst many women still wear traditional costumes as a matter of course. The best known of these is a blue woollen skirt with hand-painted floral designs, a hand-coloured smock (known as a 'kraplap' or 'kroplap'), a chequered shawl and a white tuft bonnet, which was worn to church. The women of Zuid-Beveland in Zeeland generally dressed more expressively. Their costumes were characterised by the large, spreading lace bonnet with bright golden stitches pressed against the back of the head, a thick red coral necklace and a silver chatelaine bag fastened to their waistbands. In many regions, such as the Achterhoek, the costume was less extravagant, which reflected the material limitations of those communities. When all is said and done, the loss of the traditional costume has certainly contributed to the loss of variety that made our country so vibrant.

Today, these picturesque little houses, built by true craftsmen many, many years ago, can only be found in the southern-most tip of the Netherlands in the rolling hills of the province of Limburg. Sadly the postmasters' lovely hand-painted information boards are a thing of the past.

112 *Farms and Traditional Costumes*

The layout of the old farmlands in, for example, the east of Holland, is quite different from the flat, treeless polder lands. Even the boundaries of the old pastures are demarcated by rows of trees or lovely wooded banks. These old landscapes provide a rich and varied habitat for a wide range of flora and fauna.

Farms and Traditional Costumes

Pages 114 and 115:
The sunset is spectacular in the damp and misty pastoral landscape – romantic for some, inspiring for others!

The Dutch pollard willow can withstand its fair share of pushing and shoving. It tolerates regular pollarding for firewood, and yields the weaving materials for baskets, and matting used in dike improvement works. It is the pollarding that lends it the characteristic gnarled appearance. The wood of the pollard willow is also used to make wooden clogs. These hardy trees are also capable of surviving serious flooding due to the fact that they can survive under water, root and all, for extended periods of time.

Nature & Nostalgia

Chapter 8

Clogs and Cheese

A few chapters ago, I wrote that, for centuries, foreigners saw Holland as the land of windmills. But Holland is also the land of wooden clogs. Even today, farmers continue to wear wooden clogs; albeit to a lesser extent than in the past. In earlier days clogs were not limited to the rural areas; fishermen around the Zuiderzee wore them onboard, and in the last century workers still wore them in cities and in towns. While, to foreigners this was one of the unique characteristic of the Netherlands, local city dwellers described clog-wearing country people as 'het klompenvolkje' or 'clog-wearing country folk' - a somewhat derogatory upper class reference to the common people.

Clogs were hand crafted and, if the buyer had the time to wait, the clog maker would make them to measure. Every town had its own clog maker and, as in the case of the farmsteads and costumes, here there were marked traditions too. The Noord-Holland clog, the Zeeland clog, the Frisian clog, the Noord-Brabant clog and the Overijssel clog - they were all slightly different. Clog designs could even differ from town to town. They could differ in shape, colour and embellishment - all of which was achieved with painting and carving techniques. Moreover, the specific design of the clog could be functional in the sense that it belonged to professional in a specific branch of industry.

Every Region had its Own Clog Designs

The handcrafted clogs of Marken and Hindeloopen were particularly interesting, the latter village being renowned for its artistically painted furniture and clogs. Everyone had (at least) one set of clogs for the week and a special pair for Sundays. Church clogs in Hindeloopen were beautifully decorated with biblical scenes. In Marken clogs were hand painted with floral designs and young betrothed women wore particularly elegant clogs with hand-carved rosettes, miracle buttons, and charming entwined hearts. Sometimes the wedding date was painted on the clogs. The clog makers of the town of Purmerend manufactured simple, lightweight clogs that were ideal for hiking.

The people of the province of Noord-Brabant also liked painted clogs. To this day, St Oedenrode remains a well-known centre of clog manufacturers. However, today's clogs are no longer tailor made – they are factory produced and ready-to-wear.

At the beginning of the 20th century clog makers in Noord-Brabant produced the so-called wooden shoe – a clog with the external appearance of a shoe, complete with painted holes for shoelaces. The village of Enter in Overijssel is still a clogmaker's centre; in this case, a fact born of necessity. The region's smallholders, each of whom possessed little more than a cow, a goat and a few sheep, needed to earn a little extra income and were able to do so by weaving fabrics on commission for textile traders (which is how the textile industry was born), and they made clogs for a pittance. Almost the entire village was involved in the clog-making industry. Remarkably, in spite of the poignant situation of the villagers, the clogs were rather elaborate in design. The town still produces clogs, albeit by machine, but still in the old design.

Brightly painted clogs, a barrel organ and the cheese girl always stir the tourist imagination.

To School in Clogs

Children in rural areas also wore clogs – they even went to school in clogs. However, at school, just like at home, all clogs had to be left at the door before sitting down in the classroom with friends. The lid of the school desk could be opened to keep books and other belongings; in early days it was a slate and slate pencils that were kept in a slate-pencil box. Later, students used steel pens to write on paper, and the Dutch dip pen became renowned all over the world. A glass inkpot was sunk into the desktop, so the pen could be dipped into the ink from time to time. That process would be almost unimaginable for the ballpoint pen generation of today.

In 1900, Dutch legislation made school education compulsory. Today, Dutch children receive the highest number of daily educational hours in the world. Compared to most other countries, a major proportion of that time is spent learning foreign languages. Naturally, you need smart teachers to produce smart children.

120 *Clogs and Cheese*

Children's Games were Fun

Do children still play outside, or do they spend all their free time on the computer? In days gone by there were lots of things to do outside; there was the clog dance, for example, and a host of other games. Some had been past down from generation to generation for centuries. One such game was playing with the hoop – Roman children, too, were fond of playing this game. Then there was the game of knucklebones, also known as 'playing dibs', which was played with the bones of a sheep's foot. Does anybody still play skipping games today? And hopscotch; which was played mainly by girls - they used to draw squares on the pavement, throw stones into the squares, and perform an intricate hopping ritual based on a code of strict rules. The children of the late Middle Ages had already mastered the art of blowing bubbles, and they enjoyed playing blind man's buff, leapfrog and stilt walking. Until recently children still played marbles, spinning top, prisoner's base, touch, hide and seek, and all around the mulberry bush. Do they still play any of those games today? Computer games are fascinating, but a healthy round of outdoor games never hurt anyone.

Some alternative education in clog dancing may come in handy one day.

Clogs and Cheese

The Clog Dance – Energetic, yet Civilised

On the whole, the Dutch are a modest people; a fact that is beautifully illustrated by the clog dance. Clog dancing in Holland is a series of cautious and apparently well thought-out dancing manoeuvres. However, I believe there is another, rather practical explanation for this: If you dance too wildly, you might just lose your clogs.

Strangely enough, the old-fashioned Dutch clog dance shares many elements with the modern jive - only much more civilised. It also resembles an American line dance –thought-through, synchronised steps, rehearsed to perfection. The clog dance was a colourful affair that was mostly performed at village fairs where everyone was decked out in their most colourful and festive best. And the children danced along. The music, performed on the piano accordion, the barrel organ, and the washboard for rhythm, may not always have been the most exciting, but it was almost invariably played from the heart. Come to think of it, Dutch farmers and fishermen used to throw pretty good parties.

Pages 122 and 123:
The clog dance – catch them when they're young!

Cheese Making is a Thousand Years Old

Many years ago, archaeologists discovered two earthen plates, with small holes in the bottom, on a Frisian terp. The plates closely resembled the wooden cheese vats farmer's wives used under the cheese press to remove excess whey and to shape the cheese. Those wooden vats, too, have small holes underneath. The Frisian terps were made between 500 BC and 1,000 AD, which implies that the art of making durable products from milk is an ancient art. So clearly Dutch cheese has been around for a long, long time.

Every town has its own typical dancing style; driven on by the pumping sound of the barrel organ and accordion, and the beat of the washboard.

Clogs and Cheese

Cheese was an Export Product in Medieval Times

The simplest technique employed to make cheese in the olden days was to let the milk turn thick and sour, and to collect the solids in a cloth. Once all liquid had dripped out, the residue was a soft white mass of cheese – a simple recipe with names such as curds ('wrongel'), 'hangebast' and ooze ('dikke prut'). Today, this ancient delicacy is known as cottage cheese. But the Dutch have also been making hard cheeses ever since the Middle Ages. We know that they shipped hard Frisian, Leidse, Edammer and Gouda cheeses to England, France and Spain in medieval times. Strangely enough, the Dutch themselves were not big cheese and butter eaters in those early days. Butter was considered a luxury (and still is to some extent), and butter and cheese could never be eaten together. A common caution against such indulgence was: 'Zuivel op zuivel is het werk van de duivel', which translates roughly to: 'Dairy on dairy is the work of the devil'.

The Farmer's Wife is the Cheese Maker

Prior to the establishment of the first, small cheese factory in Waddinxveen, all Dutch cheese was produced on the farm. Today this is still the case on at least a thousand Dutch farms. Farm cheese is extremely popular due to the fact that it generally has a more characteristic flavour than factory-made cheese. This is mainly because the farmers do not pasteurise the raw milk before processing it. Cheese making is a labour-intensive, time-consuming craft, which was, and remains to this day, the exclusive domain of the farmer's wife. The skills have been passed down from mother to daughter throughout the centuries, and the techniques have hardly changed in all that time.

In effect, cheese making is little more than the act of separating the solids in the milk from the liquids. Dairy milk consists of 87% water – the remainder is the solids that are used to make cheese. Cheese is certainly healthy – after all, the solids contain all the milk's fats, proteins, minerals and vitamins. Essentially, cheese is formed by an ancient coagulant that derives from the fourth stomach of the newborn calf. The coagulant, with lactic acid bacteria, is added to the milk, and enzymes cause the lactic protein in the milk to form lumps – it coagulates. A host of other ingredients are added and, finally, once the whey has been drained, the curds that are left behind are pressed into recognisable cheese shapes. Finally the cheese is preserved in a salt bath and kept to dry.

Holland: The Land of Cheese!

Cheese making in the factory is essentially the same as on the farm, with one important difference; the milk is pasteurised. However, presently some factory-made cheeses are treated more naturally, whereby fewer bacteria are eliminated. The flavours of those cheeses more closely resemble those of the authentic farm cheeses. The advent of the dairy factory, at the beginning of the 20th century, was stimulated by the dairy farmers themselves when they formed the first dairy cooperatives, many of which are still in existence today. It is a near certainty that the small cheese farmer could never have created sufficient supply to satisfy the growing demand for cheese. In 1998 the Netherlands produced more than six hundred thousand tons of cheese, with the volume of Gouda being the greatest. With cheese being one of our most important export products, it is clear that, indeed, Holland is a land of cheese.

Saying 'Holland' is like saying, 'Cheese!' Dutch cheese is renowned all over the world, and the appreciation of our cheese is evident from the annual sales figures. The cheese trade is a high-paced industry; as is evident from these cheese bearers sprinting back and forth across the market. You need a solid sense of balance, because the idea is to make the money roll, not the cheese! Authentic Dutch cheese is available from most dairy farms, where extensive selections are always on display. A little taste of everything makes it easier to decide – or does it? A cheese farmer explains the various cheeses and production methods.

Clogs and Cheese

The willow is an extremely useful tree. Its shoots are used for all kinds of weaving - from fences to shopping baskets. In the pale light of the setting winter sun, the spears change hue from bright yellow to deep orange.

Few of these fields remain today, and this natural produce, too, is being replaced by the growing use of industrially manufactured materials.

Nature & Nostalgia

The Advent of the Mixed Farm

Going back to the Iron Age, in about 800 (years) BC, man invented something that is still around today - the wooded bank. The wooded bank was known as the 'Celtic Fields' due to the fact that it was an agricultural style invented by the Celts. This approach to crop cultivation was later practised in the province of Drenthe. It consisted of small patches of land hedged in by wooded banks created from the trunks of felled trees and travelled stones moved here by glaciers in the Ice Age. The wooded banks yielded a remarkably intensive crop.

As early as the Bronze Age, man discovered the value of adding manure to the soil – an event that heralded in the age of mixed farming. Before that, crop cultivation and animal husbandry were separate industries. In those days it was not uncommon for a farmer to have 50 head of cattle. It is assumed that, due to the success of this intensive style of farming, and the resulting larger population, farmers began to move away to the tidal marshes of Groningen and Friesland, among other places. Conditions were, of course, very different in those regions, which gave rise to the first terp settlements, where animal husbandry (cattle and sheep) became the dominant industry. Trading followed in later years and, by the early Middle Ages, the Frisians had established themselves as sailors and traders par excellence. Of course, wherever there are cows, goats or sheep, there is cheese and butter. Old Frisian terps have yielded components of tools, such as those used to churn butter, which supports this theory.

132 *Agriculture, Crop Cultivation and Livestock*

In the past, man made the most of nature's own supplies; such as ducks, snails and honey. Where there were wild flowers, there would usually be honey close by. It demanded a certain amount of effort to harvest the honey; but so did trapping ducks. It certainly is easier to get hold of them once they are inside the duck decoy. The traps are located at the converging point of numerous ditches. The decoy man depended on his trusty decoy dog to get the ducks from the ponds into the ditches. The alert, but unsuspecting ducks follow the dog into the trap while keeping a watchful eye on him. The decoy man watches patiently from behind the reeds – once the ducks are close enough, he leaps up and chases them down the funnel and into the trap. Duck decoys are no longer used as traps – they have been converted into natural islands that host a range of rare plants and animals.

Agriculture, Crop Cultivation and Livestock

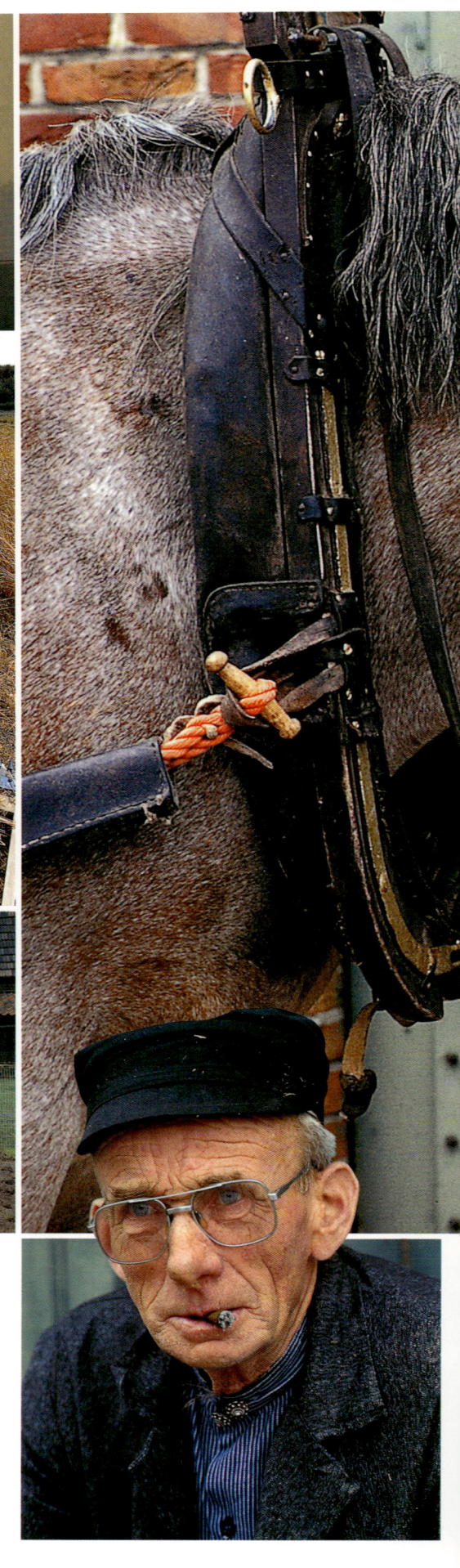

No Arable Land, No Agriculture

Early agriculture, even as late as the Middle Ages, would have been unimaginable without prior cultivation of the land. Settlers in terrains with sandy soil were forced to clear forests and heaths, and colonists of marshy peat bogs had to drain the land before being able to start crop cultivation.

Most of the wild areas had formerly been claimed by big landowners, known as Lords of the Domain, such as counts and lower ranking nobility. To convert the land to arable soil, they needed farmers. In the early and later Middle Ages those farmers were serfs, such as slaves, serfs and free farmers, all of whom were to a greater or lesser extent dependant on their lords and masters. This was the time of the One Tenth Law, a law originally invented by the church, which was later adopted by secular rulers. The 'free' serfs worked their masters' land as well as their own parcel of land, on which they cultivated produce for their own and their families' sustenance. It was here that the One Tenth Law applied: Ten percent of the total yield of the land was destined for the landlord – in other words, one tenth of all newborn lambs, one tenth of all fowl, one tenth of the grain harvest, one tenth of all fruit, and so on. In the later Middle Ages this extreme dependence on the landlord decreased, especially when currency became freely available and the leasehold system was introduced.

134   *Agriculture, Crop Cultivation and Livestock*

In the past, a horse was both a valuable and indispensable asset on every farm. They were used as beasts of burden, as draught animals and as means of transport, and could be found working the field day in and day out.

Horse driving is an underestimated art; as is maintenance of the harness and all related things. The farmer worked long, hard days to harvest the land and get the produce to the market in time.

Agriculture, Crop Cultivation and Livestock

Farmers Created the Dutch Landscape

It is interesting to note that, to this day, ancient cultivation practises determine the character of almost every contemporary Dutch landscape. This is particularly true in the peat lands where, to protect their land against the water, farmers were forced to build dikes around large tracts of land. The first records of this labour date back to the year 1,000. To drain the land, the farmer would dig ditches around parcels of land allocated to him by his landlord. In Noord-Overijssel,

near Staphorst and Rouveen, colonists were free to extend their land as far the peat permitted – in many cases the lots were (and still are) several kilometres long, with farmstead located at the top of the land. A similar trend developed in the Dutch peat lands known as the 'Hollandveen'. In the latter instance, though, the cultivation process, known as the 'Great Cultivation' was arranged by a higher hand – the Count or Bishop issued cultivation concessions whereby the length and width of the parcel was determined in advance. Such a concession was known as a 'cope', and some local town names still refer to that system, e.g. Boskoop and Nieuwkoop. An aerial view of the landscape best reveals the long, straight and highly regular parcels of land.

To get the most out of the lean and rugged soil in the central and eastern regions of the country, farmers grazed sheep and goats on the land. When the land failed to yield the necessary nutrition, the waste food collector saved the day. Today, however, all peels and food waste products are disposed of by the garbage collector, and nutritional supplements must be found elsewhere for the natural foragers.

Agriculture, Crop Cultivation and Livestock

Farmlands were maintained by any means available

Most of the farmers that settled in Hollandveen originated from the higher sandy regions where they had practised crop and livestock farming. Naturally, they would have tried to practise their old ways here. However, the land was wet and unstable, so they were compelled to use a lightweight horse instead of an ox to draw their ploughs. Perhaps, here, as in Twente, farmers also practised the 'three-field system', whereby the farmer would divide his land into three sections; one for winter grains (rye and wheat), one for summer grains (oats and barley) or legumes, while the third section remained untilled. Using this system, as well as the 'four-field system' (both of which are still in use today), the use of land would be rotated on an annual basis.

Due, mainly, to settling of the land, the soil became permanently wet and increasingly less suitable for agricultural purposes. Once it was no longer possible to drain the land, due to the fact that the polder lay below the level of the surrounding water (as is still the case today), it became necessary to introduce the windmills.

Agriculture, Crop Cultivation and Livestock

Eventually crop cultivation simply became an unattainable ambition and those areas were used only for livestock farming, with cheese and milk as principle products. Thanks to the enormous effort of those early farmers who maintained the dikes, the sluices, the mills, the watercourses and the quays, this remains essentially unchanged today.

Large sections of the Netherlands have indeed been reclaimed. A task of such scope could only have been attained by collective initiative. This collective effort gave rise to phenomena called the Polder Boards, which regulate and control all related activities. One rule that was observed for a long, long time, dictated that every farmer would be responsible for the section of dike immediately adjacent to his land. However, not all farmers observed the rule and, as a result, many dike banks broke in those early days.

There is less demand today for the straight and monotonous rows of production plantations. These old forests are being 'neglected' systematically in order to render them more natural. The new nature policy is designed to promote natural diversity. Dead wood is left to decompose naturally, and felled trees are not replaced in order to allow forests to regenerate spontaneously. Alien cattle species have been imported to encourage varied growth through grazing. Although they need supplementary fodder in winter, hardy Scottish Highlanders can survive all four seasons in rugged terrain. It's a rare experience to encounter one of these animals in a Dutch forest or heath.

Agriculture, Crop Cultivation and Livestock

Valuable Dutch dairy cows spend their winters in the stalls to prevent irregular dairy production. Prior to going to market, they are thoroughly washed and combed. The farmer will do everything possible to fetch the highest possible price for his cow.

As Cities Grew, Farmers Produced for Markets

Originally, all farmers were subsistence farmers. Medieval farmers struggled severely under the one-tenth laws, whereby major portions of their yields were claimed by landlords. However, as the cities grew, those farmers began to produce for local markets. The demand created by the local markets determined the nature of the farmers business. And that demand was dictated by the needs and desires of industry and consumers in the cities, which, in turn, resulted in a broad diversity of agricultural production. Cheese had long since become a market item, and while around the 14th century there may not have been many cheese maidens around, Holland had already become an important cheese-exporting country. Every region in the country had its own specialities targeting specific markets. Those markets included madder and woad that were grown to create dyes for the textile industry, flax for the linen industry, hops and barley for breweries, hemp for the rope makers, rapeseed for the oil mills, vegetables, and especially fruit (it was con-

The inspector, on the other hand, judges the cow on more than mere outward appearance. Once all data have been exchanged about the cow, buyer and seller will start an intricate bargaining ritual characterised by an alternating series of shouts and hand-claps that is consummated in a mutually acceptable price. The initial amounts differ substantially, but every new clap brings them a little closer to a compromise, and a deal.

sidered chic), and beef, which a popular item in the late Middle Ages. There were even companies that fattened cattle imported from Denmark for the market. Most of those companies were located near the cities and along the IJssel River. While farmers continued to till the land well after the Middle Ages, much had changed. Fertilisers were introduced in the 19th century, advanced agricultural machinery was used to work the land, auctions system replaced markets, and dairy factories replaced home industries. All that not withstanding, at its core, the agricultural industry is still the same today as it always was.

Although the Dutch love farming, not everyone can be a real farmer. Fortunately allotment gardens allow everyone to work his or her own little patch of land in their own free time. Sometimes the weather plays up, as in the case of the town of Tollebeek in the province of Flevoland. Once, during a particularly heavy downpour, the accumulated rain on the polder found its natural way to the lowest point in the local geography – the centre of the village. The town was flooded under a deluge of half a metre of water. Neither the water pump nor the sandbags could prevent the crop of onions and vegetables from going to waste. The lesson? Never build a town at the lowest point on the polder! Needless to say, that practise has since been rooted out.

142 *Agriculture, Crop Cultivation and Livestock*

Generally, new polder land is immediately seeded with cabbage seeds. In May, spectacular fields of yellow cabbage flowers stretch out as far as the eye can see.

Nature & Nostalgia 143

Pages 144 and 145:
On experimental farms, such as this one, the grower will select only the most beautiful and robust tulips to develop into commercial crops.

Commercial flower bulb growers will do everything in their power to offer customers the greatest possible variety of shapes and colours.

146 *Nature & Nostalgia*

Chapter 10

Homage to the Tulip

There is an official international registry where the names of every conceivable type of tulip that ever existed have been recorded – a list of no less than 2,700 names. No other country on earth is more directly responsible for the enormous variety of tulips in existence today than Holland. Foreign tourists understandably view Holland as the Land of the Tulip. Strangely enough, few Dutch actually realise that the bulb season, in April and May, is the high season of the local tourist industry. Of course there are other well-known bulbous plants that bloom in spring too; the narcissus, the daffodil and the hyacinth, to name a few. Tourists annually delight in vast vistas of flower fields that extend as far as the eye can see, as well as in the gardens of Keukenhof. The tulip is by far the most important of these flowers and makes up 25% of the more than five million bulbous flowers exported by the Netherlands each year.

The Tulip comes from Turkey

It is quite remarkable that this incredibly flourishing industry probably began in 1570 with one or two unattractive tulip bulbs obtained from such distant climes as Turkey or North-east Greece. There are many contradictory stories about exactly how those bulbs found their way onto Dutch shores. Moreover, the tulip may well have originated even farther away, in places such as Persia (Iran), where its beauty was praised in verses dating back to the 12th century. The tulip was also viewed as a precious commodity in the courts of the Ottoman (Turkish) sultans in Constantinople.

The Tulip Mania of 1634 to 1637

We do know with reasonable certainty that Carolus Clusius (the learned liked to adopt Latin names in those days) started tulip growing in Leiden towards the end of the 16th century. The industry grew with rapid strides and by 1612 a trader named Emanuel Sweerts was already exporting tulips to Germany. France, too, showed a robust interest in the flower: In the '20s and '30s of the 17th century, ladies-in-waiting in the court of Louis XIII considered the tulip the preferred flower to receive from admirers.

It is quite likely that this aristocratic interest led to the Tulip Mania that raged from 1634 to 1637. It was the sort of industry that could quite reasonably be compared to a certain branch of equity trading in our own times – pure speculation. Everyone took part, and most of the (actual) trading occurred in inns. It soon assumed the character of a futures trade. People signed contracts on the basis of bulbs they did not own yet, and prices went through the roof. The most popular tulips were those with striped and flaming flowers - a regular feature in 17th century Dutch still life paintings. Probably the most popular was the yellow-red flaming tulip, which, ironically, owed its extravagant colour scheme to a natural virus infection.

Tulip buyers spent money like water; a mere bulb of the famed 'Semper Augustus', a brown tulip with yellow stripes, was worth up to NLG 10,000! For the same amount one could at that time, buy a stately canal house in Amsterdam – obviously, in retrospect, a far better investment, as that speculative industry collapsed abruptly in 1737 when the Dutch Government put an end to it.

Multicoloured ribbons of flower fields breathe new life into old dairy pastures, and attract millions of tourists every year. A genuine Delft Blue tulip vase is a thing of rare beauty.

Painters were fascinated by the Tulip

As mentioned above, the tulip's popularity in the past is reflected in the art of the time. There were also many specialised books on tulips, many of them with exquisite representations, produced on commission by traders to support their sales. Obviously, after the period known as Tulip Mania, the real industry continued.

A particularly famous tulip painting was created by Judith Leyster in 1643. Images of tulips are also found on colourful house tiles in many old Dutch homes. Alexandre Dumas (1802 –1870) immortalised the tulip in his literary work, 'The Black Tulip'. Black tulips, by the way, are not really all that special – they are quite easily created by pouring a little black pigment on the flower as soon as it appears, or by keeping it in a dark room.

Tulips Flourish all over the Netherlands

Most Dutch know that the tulip is grown in sandy 'geest' soils found between the sand dunes and the polder; however, tulip cultivation can also be highly successful in completely different types of soil. This expansionist trend began south of Haarlem in the sixteenth century, and grew towards the south to an area known as the bulb-growers region. The sandy and sand-clay soils are enormously well suited to the plants and the temperate maritime climate and the light salty quality of the air limit the incidence of plant lice - the scourge of all growers. Other important bulb-growing areas are located north of Haarlem, at the top of Noord-Holland, in West Friesland, and even on the island of Texel.

148   *Homage to the Tulip*

Fields of tulips stretch out as far as the eye can see. One of the prettiest features of this fascinating industry is the experimental farms where growers experiment incessantly with new types, colours and shapes of flowers. Unfortunately there is a negative side to this - the herbicides used by growers to destroy poorly formed and coloured plants form a direct assault on the environment. Hopefully, genetic modification will soon put an end to this practise and relieve the environment of this burden.

Homage to the Tulip

152　*Homage to the Tulip*

Homage to the Tulip

Pages 152 and 153:
Keukenhof is situated on the former 15th century hunting grounds of Jacoba van Beieren; undoubtedly, today, these fields are 'happier hunting grounds' than they were in former times.

A barrier bars entry to buses and other vehicles where formerly luxurious coaches rattled down tree-lined lanes. Refuse bins are placed strategically in an attempt to keep the forest clean.

Normally, in nature, only a single species truly benefits from a monotonous landscape, and it is rare for it to bloom en masse.
Dandelions thrive on the fertile soils that formerly constituted the seabed.

The first flower to make its appearance in early spring is the lovely little snowdrop.

156 *Nature & Nostalgia*

Chapter 11

Flowers and Greenhouses

For years, 'Say it with flowers' was the principal motto of the Dutch flower industry. However, are we always sure exactly what we are saying when offering someone a bouquet of flowers? Certainly we know that in most instances the receiver will appreciate the gesture. In most instances what we are probably trying to say is something like, 'I like you'. However, traditionally certain types of flowers conveyed certain, very specific messages. Unfortunately most of us, today, no longer know exactly what those messages are and the flowers they are associated with. Sadly that language has been largely lost to us. The freesia represented innocence, the iris wisdom, the lily purity, and the forget-me-not represented true love. Throughout the ages the violet expressed a secret love for the receiver, while the rose has been the absolute expression of love and beauty for thousands of years. Without a doubt, the rose is the flower with the greatest erotic charge. In ancient Greece roses were associated with Aphrodite, the goddess of love. Today, the rose is the only flower whose message is still universally understood. Women are often compared to the rose, and many women around the world bear its name.

Holland, Land of Flowers

The Dutch are a sober nation; yet any book about the Netherlands must be deemed incomplete without mention of Holland's flowers. Undoubtedly most foreign visitors are impressed by the sea of flowers that bloom in Holland in spring; however, the true pride of the Dutch is the virtual explosion of colour in their own flower gardens in season.

The Netherlands may have been known as the land of clogs in the past, but today, more than any other country on earth, it is the premier land of the flowers. In many ways, it seems, the Dutch invented flowers. While not our country's largest industry, Holland is the undisputed leader in the trade in cut flowers – that industry is, quite literally, controlled by the Netherlands. Anyone buying a bouquet of flowers in Berlin, London, Rome or Tokyo has more than likely bought Dutch flowers.

The Great Revolution: Greenhouse Cultivation

How did we achieve this? Undoubtedly it is due to the phenomenon of greenhouse cultivation. Growing flowers in the open air exposes growers and their crops to excessive risks due to variable weather conditions. The use of glasshouses to eliminate that negative variable has resulted in enormous production growth. The practise of cultivating flowers in greenhouses was initiated at the same time as the cultivation of vegetables in the greenhouse. Here, too, the Netherlands is a leading player.

In a way, greenhouse cultivation was the historical consequence of fruit, vegetable and herb cultivation in the sheltered environment of walled-in vegetable gardens in convents, monasteries and castles in the Middle Ages. Horticulture, with its high yield on small areas of land, saw rapid growth around fast-growing cities. The glasshouse industry began in the 19th century, when it was discovered that glass could also be stretched – prior to that all glass products had been blown. Indoor ornamental plant cultivation accelerated around 1900 with the appearance of the first large free-standing glass houses, specifically in the Aalsmeer area - a national and global centre of flower cultivation. Another important greenhouse area is located at Westland, south of The Hague. Other smaller centres include the area north of Alkmaar, Venlo, Breda, Emmen and north of Nijmegen.

Flowering plants are highly selective, and demand intensive care and rich soil. However, picked at the right moment, they make objects of exceptional beauty. The orchid, in its infinite variety surely deserves the title of 'queen of the flowers'.

The Grower creates the Climate

The greenhouse enables the grower to eliminate the negative influence of adverse weather conditions. Stronger still, the greenhouse enables the grower to create his own climate by regulating temperature, humidity, water supply and light. While the latter element is simply determined by the amount of light penetrating the glass, some growers use artificial lights at night (something not many neighbouring residents are happy about). The grower is also able to change the nutritional quality of the soil, e.g. instead of growing in its natural medium, the plant might be grown on a synthetic substratum of mineral wool. Decorative flowers, such as the rose and geranium, are particularly fond of such layers. The grower simply adds water and nutrition; both of which are regulated by computer. The computer also determines when the ventilation windows need to be opened.

Contemporary flower cultivation has become a high-tech science indeed – with one exception; flowers are still picked manually – in that regard there is nothing, as yet, to replace the human hand.

Growing Environmental Awareness

Intensive cultivation, which is primarily oriented to high crop yields, has one major disadvantage; the plants are hypersensitive to pests, such as insects, fungi and bacteria. In the past, the grower's primary response was to deploy a range of chemical treatments or, as they used to call them, 'plant protection agents'. Fortunately biological treatment is a growing trend. Environmental protection and sustainable cultivation have become central themes in flower cultivation. This includes water recycling and smart application of the natural enemies of harmful scourges. For example, the use of Amblyseius Cucumeris against red spider mite, and the ichneumon wasp against the white fly. Another interesting, and rather poetic application is the use of the assassin or kissing bug against aphids. Admittedly the natural, biological fight against pests is most difficult in the case of decorative flowers. This is due to a host of highly exacting demands placed upon the production of decorative plants – not only the flower, but the leaf too must be perfect. These conditions do not apply to fruits, such as the cucumber and tomato. A healthier approach that is taking root reasonably quickly, is biological cultivation - a technique that completely eliminates the use of pesticides, herbicides and fertilizers. Biological cultivation is a growing force in the decorative plant industry. The most amazing measures are being deployed in the name of pest control – they include the use of nettles against aphids, sulphur against weevils (that bore holes in plants' leaves), boiled tobacco

The rose is the symbol of love, beauty and joy. Only a rose is capable of truly conveying the message of love. No wonder then that there is such a demand for their flowers. Roses are vulnerable to natural elements, but flourish in the ideal, protected environment of the greenhouse. It is an art in itself to create the perfect combination of colours in a pleasing bouquet.

Flowers and Greenhouses 159

162 *Flowers and Greenhouses*

From the auction building in Naaldwijk, an expanse of greenhouses stretches out as far as the eye can see, and beyond, as far as The Hague. There are enough greenhouses in this belt to guarantee a substantial daily supply of flowers all year round. Every available patch of earth is covered by glass and yields crops all year round, albeit somewhat less in winter than in summer due to heating costs. The ultimate destination of most of the flowers is the flower vase; however, some folks have rather unique ideas about the use of flowers.

Flowers and Greenhouses

Pages 166 and 167:
A rare sight indeed – a field of blossoming Sweet Williams beside a quiet country road in Zeeland!

Misty landscapes in the east of the country, illuminated by the low, pale wintry sun are less transparent than those in the west. In the east, too, adjacent pastures are still separated by green strips of land. However, sometimes barbed wire serves a useful purpose even in a poetic landscape such as this.

Nature & Nostalgia

Chapter 12

Winter Festivities and Fun on the Ice

There is no festival more essentially Dutch than Santa Claus or 'Sinterklaas'. In early December Sinterklaas starts to pop up everywhere. Sinterklaas' arrival by boat every year in a host of cities and towns is a veritable folk festival. Which is all the more remarkable considering Sinterklaas never really existed. That aside, in the past he used to be an extremely useful figure in the educational process, as children were led to believe in his existence for as long as possible. In the 19th and early 20th century Sinterklaas was not the kindly old chap that we know today. In fact, in those days he was the scourge of all children, as parents used to chide them with the warning; "If you don't behave, Sinterklaas will come around and take you away to Spain!" Numerous 'educational' depictions in children's books show Sinterklaas collecting naughty children and stuffing them into a bag held open by his willing assistant, Piet. On the other hand, he was also portrayed as the good child's friend: 'Obey your parents and you'll be rewarded with something nice', but woe to those who dare to disobey Mom and Dad! How did the story of 'Sinterklaas, the children's friend' begin?

Saint Nicholas, the Predecessor of Sinterklaas

The story of the origin of Sinterklaas is an interesting one, but it is rather complex. Moreover, there are two versions. The first is Germanic, and therefore a pagan tale, while the second is a Christian story. According to the Germanic version, the Sinterklaas character derives from Wotan, the principal Germanic god. Like Wotan, this Sinterklaas had a long beard, was wrapped in a large cape, carried a magical staff (or spear) and thundered about from roof to roof on his dapple steed named Sleipnir. This version is not taken very seriously.

In fact, Sinterklaas is seen as a reincarnation of Saint Nicholas, the fourth bishop of the city of Myra in the present Western Turkey. There are many legends about that particular bishop, based on which he could be the patron of all sorts of people – of sailors, for example, but also of prisoners, travellers and traders and, believe it or not, virgins in search of a lover. Relics of his latter function survive in the concepts of the lover as a gingerbread man, and hearts offered to unmarried girls until the 5th of December.

When Italian merchants took the bones of Saint Nicholas from Myra to Bari in Southern Italy, the city promptly built and dedicated a church to him. Various relics of the good saint were later distributed throughout Europe; for example, the Church of the Virgin Mary in Maastricht purportedly has one of his teeth. Saint Nicholas became a popular patron saint, specifically for sailors, which explains the existence of so many Saint Nicholas churches in port cities. In Holland there are several of these churches located in old fishing villages around the IJsselmeer. As a matter of fact, Saint Nicholas is the patron saint of Amsterdam.

Child's Best Immortal Friend

The legend of Saint Nicholas, the child's best immortal friend, originated in the north of France sometime in the Middle Ages. Legend has it that a wicked innkeeper killed three schoolboys and stuffed their bodies into a pickling vat to sell as pork (this type of legend is rarely an elevating tale). Saint Nicholas, who is immortal, brought them back to life. In any event, in medieval times, once a year in French convent schools, a child was elected to the role of bishop and assigned the task of reprimanding the other children for their conduct during the past year. This tradition spread across the whole of Europe. >

Fortunately the Dutch do not believe in hibernation, and can be relied upon to provide some fun throughout the winter. In crisp clear tones, the town crier announces the festivities; where Santa Claus (St Nicholas) and Father Christmas can buy their presents, and whether the ice is thick enough for skating.

Every year, during a festive celebration, Sinterklaas (Santa Claus), accompanied by his dapple-grey and knaves, is brought into town by steamboat. On 5 December, when Santa Claus is celebrated in the Netherlands, children eagerly unwrap their presents to the tune of the traditional "Sinterklaasje kom maar binnen met je knecht!......" ("Santa Claus, please enter with your servant..."). During this period many supermarkets dress their staff in the traditional costume of Santa's knaves, known as "Zwartepieten" or Black Peters. Children, in exchange for colour-in drawings, receive marzipan sweets, spicy biscuits known as 'pepernoten', and small presents. Night falls early during Santa

The phenomenon of the child bishop was first mentioned in Dordrecht in Holland in 1360. Also, every year since 1427, from the 5th of December (memorial day of Saint Nicholas), shoes filled with coins were placed in the Saint Nicholas Church in Utrecht for the children of the poor. Hence the Dutch children's tradition to set out a shoe for gifts from Sinterklaas.

Sinterklaas Festival only celebrated in Holland

How does one explain the fact that the Festival of Sinterklaas is celebrated nowhere other than in Holland? For that is indeed the case. This historical peculiarity can largely be blamed on the church. The Calvinists considered the tradition of Sinterklaas too worldly; after all, all gifts were blessings from the Lord Jesus Christ. However, by the time the Calvinists came along, the legend

had been too firmly ingrained into family traditions in Holland, so, unlike England and Germany, it was near impossible to root it out here. The Catholic Church also banned the celebrations, as a result of which the tradition did die out in the Catholic countries. In Holland Sinterklaas celebrations have become an expression of that which is typically Dutch, homely middle-class togetherness. And, as in the medieval French tradition, family members still playfully reprimand one another in verses based on the 'culprit's' idiosyncrasies. In England, and later in America, the tradition of handing out gifts was moved to Christmas. However, we can safely assume that the American Santa Claus is none other than an adaptation of our own Sinterklaas.

Now I would like to deal with the other big confusion associated with Sinterklaas, namely the man known as 'Zwartepiet' or Black Peter. The story goes that Saint Nicholas, as a holy man, once succeeded in vanquishing a devil that had been burnt black in the fires of hell. Based on that tale, Zwartepiet originally represented the threat from hell; however, as the belief in the existence of devils faded, the menacing black figure was conveniently transformed into the faithful servant of the good old saint. So the story goes.

Christmas is not very old

The theories about the origins of Christmas are also fraught with controversy. One popular theory concerns the pagan tale of Yuletide, according to which spirits terrified people for the duration of the twelve days around New Year. The restless spirits could only be appeased with a great deal of noise and sacrifices (gifts). The sacrifices served the additional purpose of hastening the solstice and the approaching fertility of the earth. In short, these rituals were fertility rites, which, needless to say, the church was not very happy about. However, to assign a Christian meaning to the pagan celebrations and appease the pagans, the Church set Christmas, and the birth of Christ, on the 25th of December, a date that roughly coincided with the pagan celebration of solstice. Which seems a reasonably viable theory, as socio-historical theories go.

The first cribs were seen in our country during the 14th century. In those days, the festival itself was rather an exuberant event, as the original Dutch name for Christmas Eve explains; 'dikkevretsaovond', which, in English means something like 'stuff-yourself-evening'. However, that material indulgence was banned soon after the Reformation, and there is almost no further mention of Christmas in Holland after that. The homely celebration, as we know it today, was most probably a later invention of the wealthy middle classes. The Christmas tree first appeared in Holland around 1830 – a tradition borrowed from Germany, where the decorated tree was quite common amongst the wealthy upper class-

es of the 18th century. The Christmas tree however was still rather rare in Holland until 1900, and in rural areas it was quite unheard of until 1940. Only recently has the Christmas tree culture found its way into some 70% of all living rooms in the Netherlands. So the Christmas tree could be seen as a direct descendant of the holy Germanic tree - a romantic notion, which does not make any sense at all. All that notwithstanding, Christmas today has almost certainly become the most important family celebration in the Netherlands.

Winter Festivities and Fun on the Ice Father Christmas follows on the heels of Santa Claus. Christmas is the time to find and dress a perfect little Christmas tree and to start "dreaming of a White Christmas". Whether white or not, Christmas is the perfect excuse for huddling up close to the fire, sipping spicy warm wine, and munching grilled chestnuts while singing Christmas carols. On the last night of the year, we hail in the new year with a magnificent fireworks display.

Winter Festivities and Fun on the Ice 173

Carnival: A Truly Pagan Feast

While Christmas may be a distant relic of pagan rituals, Carnival, which is celebrated at the beginning of March, is a direct outcome of pagan traditions. The aim was to drive away the evil spirits of winter by means of a hellish racket, and to celebrate the rebirth of nature in the coming spring and summer. It would also appear that a fair amount of the Roman Saturnalia rites have filtered through in the form of costume parties, drinking sprees and related indulgences. During Carnival the world is turned upside down: Men dress up as women, slaves mock their masters and so on. And that is pretty much what it still represents to this day; the Prince of the Carnival reigns supreme and the jesters say their say. The name, 'Carnival' was only established once the church became involved. In 1901, the synod of Benevento in Italy gave up its resistance to the celebrations and adopted the Carnival in the liturgy; however, only 'on condition' that the feast would be preceded by a fast. The word carnival

more than likely derived from the Latin 'carne vale', which means something to the effect of 'delivery from the flesh'. Or worse still, delivery from our sins. Catholics are expected to abstain from meat for 40 days after Ash Wednesday. For their part, the Calvinist ministers of North Holland successfully managed to root out the pagan celebrations in their regions for a long, long time. However, that is a thing of the past too, as Carnival, which was always considered to be a typical Limburg and Noord-Brabant festival, is now also celebrated in the north as is made evident by the Carnival Societies that have sprung up all around the country.

You know you're well into the new year by the time the Carnival comes around. Carnival is more or less the birthright of the southerners in Holland. There's something truly liberating about getting dressed up and adopting a completely different identity for a few days. A crazy, over-the-top procession of floats forms the highlight of the festival. Key to this celebration is that everyone assumes a different identity; so everyone is everyone else's equal for those few days. The interpersonal warmth generated by this event is cause sufficient to drive the sombre northerners down to the south in droves.

Winter Festivities and Fun on the Ice

When Holland freezes over, the Dutch go Skating

Forgive me if this is starting to sound a little boring: Holland is the land of mills, the land of flowers, the land of the clog and now it is also the land of the ice skaters. As soon as the waters freeze over, the ponds, canals and ditches are invaded by skaters.

Undoubtedly ice-skating is the most common sport in the Netherlands. It is also an ancient tradition here. Ice skates made of bone have been found in Frisian terps dating back to approximately the 6th century. In fact, they were ice gliders rather than real skates and the wearer would use sticks to propel himself forward. Real skating has been around since the 14th century. Based on descriptions, we know that the skates in those days were metal gliders. By the 16th and 17th centuries skating had become a national sport as witnessed in the paintings of Hendrick Avercamp, where everyone, rich or poor, could be seen frolicking about on the ice. Another device visible in some of the paintings is the long bucket sleigh that was pulled by horses. The sleigh was also used by members of the Jester's Guild to perform tricks; hence the evolution of the pretty, painted Jester's sleighs, which were often designed in the shape of an animal, such as a lion or a swan. Another popular type of sleigh was the children's 'pricker sleds', which were invariably embellished with pretty designs. An example of this type of sleigh has survived in Hindeloopen. They were common along the entire coast of the Zuiderzee and, again, each town had its own unique version.

The minute the ice is thick enough to skate on lakes and ditches, every right-thinking Dutchman straps on his skates and takes to the ice. Undoubtedly viruses abound on those icy days; not the least of which is the virus known as the "Elfstedentocht" or Eleven City Race. This popular skating race is run along frozen canals and lakes linking eleven Frisian towns. Experienced ice officials establish the thickness of the ice at a number of strategic points along the eleven cities route to determine the start of the race. This is an essential procedure, as thousands of skaters set off over the 200-kilometre course. Sadly our temperate maritime climate makes the race somewhat of a rare event. In earlier times, the race was run on traditional Frisian skates; nowadays those old skates are mostly used as wall decorations.

176 *Winter Festivities and Fun on the Ice*

Skating On Hot Toddies

The modern racing skater could never do without 'cake and soup' stalls for a pick-me-upper, cup of soup or hot chocolate. His skating ancestors also enjoyed their pepper-uppers; only, they had a choice of steaming 'boerenkoffie' (farmer's coffee), which was nothing other than hot beer with brandy, sugar and cinnamon, anise milk and so on. The cake and soup stopovers, which also served as (illegal) gambling parlours, have been around since the 17th century.

Wooden skates were produced in Holland until the 19th century. Every town had its skate making

team consisting of the blacksmith who made the metal skate and the carpenter who made the wooden section known as the 'foot stock'. In Holland, skates were designed for gliding, while Frisian skates were specifically designed for serious racing. Records show that the first skating races were held before the year 1500. A lot of experimentation with skate designs was conducted over the years, especially the wooden racing varieties; however, the Norwegian metal tube skates finally triumphed around the end of the 19th century. In 1893, the renowned Jaap Eden became world champion on the kind of skates that are still used locally in countless racing tours run during particularly icy winters. The most famous of those races is the renowned Frisian 'Elfstedentocht' or Eleven Cities Race, the first of which was run in 1909 in a time of 13.50 hours, while the most recent race was run in 1998. The winner of that race completed the course in seven hours!

Winter Festivities and Fun on the Ice

Nature in the Netherlands

Dutch weather is as changeable as its nature and landscapes are varied. This is quite remarkable actually for a country that is so small and flat. The highest point in Holland, the Vaalserberg in Zuid-Limburg, is no more than 300 metres high. The extensive natural variation is largely due to the varying soil types, which include peat moor, high moor peat, clay, sand and loess (in Zuid-Limburg). Each soil type generates its own natural ecology. The west and the north, and the large river regions are dominated by flat pastures, cultivated land and water, while the eastern, central and southern regions are characterised by flowing hills and forests. The west of Holland and the West Frisian Islands are protected from the sea by sand dunes, which directly determine the character of those landscapes. The sandy beaches at the foot of the dunes stretch along almost the entire length of the North Sea coast from the Zeeland/Flanders border to Den Helder in the north, to the West Frisian Islands, which can only be described as jewels of natural beauty.

West-Holland and Friesland are both either partially or wholly located below sea level, while the West lies below the water level of all the rivers and canals that criss-cross the region. This explains one of the most characteristic element of the landscapes of the Netherlands - the dikes that surround the polders – large tracts of land that were once manually reclaimed from the waters that formerly dominated the land. As can be seen in the IJsselmeer and the islands of Zeeland, there is plenty of water in the Netherlands. Zeeland simply has to be one of the prettiest marriages of land and sea. All of the land in Zeeland and around the IJsselmeer (formerly known as the Zuiderzee) is shielded from water by the dikes.

The landscape undergoes major changes as one leaves the coast behind and travels towards the interior. While many of the regions in the interior, including large sections of Noord-Brabant, are still relatively flat, the southeastern tip of Noord-Holland, Het Gooi, and the Utrecht areas consist of gently undulating hills covered with forests and heaths. Further inland, in areas such as Kootwijk, and the Drunense Duinen in Noord-Brabant, one comes across the sand drift areas. Heaths can be found in the regions of the Veluwe, Drenthe and Noord-Limburg. There are presently about 17 flocks of sheep in the Netherlands.

The forests are not always equally varied; sometimes they are downright dull; long stretches of pine and spruce trees, for example. However, there are plenty of broad-leafed forests with, among others, beech trees and oaks to make up for that. The oak forests in the east of the country, for example, are the pride of the province of Drenthe, while in the area know as the Veluwezoom one can actually get lost in seemingly endless expanses of beech forest. There are also large tracts of broad-leafed forests on the Utrechtse Heuvelrug, the Veluwe and in Midden-Limburg.

Still, even here in the interior it is impossible to completely get away from the water. Talk of variety! The delta landscape in the interior is sliced up by great rivers, such as the Maas, Waal, Rhine and IJssel; all of which are hemmed in by dikes and provide some of the most beautiful sights in the country. Other stunning features are the characteristic pollard willows and, in the Betuwe, extensive stretches of fruit trees that are a joy to behold during the blossom season in spring. There are also plenty of streams in the higher sandy grounds in the southern and eastern regions of the country, in Twente, the Achterhoek and in Limburg. There are winding creeks surrounded by idyllic landscapes competing for the traveller's attention with wide green pastures, fields of flowers and clumps of trees. There are marshland areas, such as those in the lake lands at Peel in Noord-Brabant, the Weerribben in Overijssel, and the lake lands of Drenthe.

Zuid-Limburg is perhaps the most unusual region of the Netherlands. It has even been called un-Dutch due to its pretty rolling hills, forests and fast flowing creeks.

In all honesty, it must be added that the vast majority of Dutch landscapes were created by man through his intensive effort to cultivate the land. While there is water everywhere, and forests and heaths, most of the country is dominated by pastures and cultivated land. Noord-Groningen and Oost-Holland are characterised by cultivated land, while Friesland, Zeeland, Zuid- and Noord-Holland and the river regions are dominated by pastures. Man shaped the course of nearly every river in the Netherlands, partly for economic reasons, but in recent years also for more idealistic reasons, namely to protect and renew our unique natural heritage. Personally, I am overjoyed by this development. In the first place, the number of national parks has grown by leaps and bounds – there are currently ten, and that number will double in the not-too-distant future. The work being done to restore our natural heritage to its former glory is equally fascinating. Farmland is being restored to natural land in areas such as 'De Blauwe Kamer' in the river forelands along the Rhine at Rhenen, 'De Vossenberg' in Drenthe, 'De Duursche Waarden' along the IJssel River near Deventer, and many more. Some of those nature reserves cross dikes to create landscapes with wet grasslands, marshes and hardy riverine forests. Most of the maintenance work in the new nature areas is left to large alien grazers, such as Konic ponies, Scottish Highlanders and Galloway cattle from Scotland. These 'untouched' forests also attract animals naturally, such as large flocks of water bird, including the widgeon, the great crested grebe, the marsh warbler, the common tern and the stilt-walker. In the grasslands, there are geese, black-tailed godwits, redshanks and lapwings. Generally speaking, it would be fair to say that nature is thriving in most of the Netherlands.

Pages 178 and 179:
Straight roads, straight walls, straight ditches, straight trees; Holland may have a wide variety of unique characteristics, but it likes to keep a straight face!

The National parks of the Netherlands
by province

Noord Holland	Nationaal park Zuid-Kennemerland Nationaal park Duinen van Texel [under dev.]
Friesland	Nationaal park Schiermonnikoog Nationaal park Oude Venen [under dev.]
Groningen	Nationaal park Lauwersmeer [under dev.]
Drenthe	Nationaal park Dwingelderveld Nationaal park Drents-Friese Wold [under dev.] Nationaal park Drentse Aa [under dev.]
Overijssel	Nationaal park Weerribben Nationaal park De Sallandse Heuvelrug [under dev.]
Gelderland	Nationaal Park Hoge Veluwe Nationaal Park Veluwe Zoom
Utrecht	Nationaal park Utrechtse Heuvelrug [under dev.]
Zeeland	Nationaal park Oosterschelde [under dev.]
Noord Brabant	Nationaal park Groote Peel Nationaal park Biesbosch Nationaal park Loonse and Drunense Duinen [under dev.] Nationaal park De Zoom-Kalmthoutse Heide [under dev.]
Limburg	Nationaal park Hamert (Maasduinen) Nationaal park Meinweg
Flevoland	-
Zuid Holland	-

Nature & Nostalgia

Chapter 8 — *The most important sights and attraction around clogs, cheese and traditional costumes.*

Regular clog dancing and costume shows are held throughout the Netherlands. This keeps the tradition alive, as costumes are rarely worn in daily life.

Cheese and Clog Markets: Alkmaar, April through September on Fridays / Gouda, from June to September on Thursdays / Woerden, on Wednesdays / Edam / Schagen.

Clog Museums: Noardburgum / Eelde / Enter / Goor / Keijenborg / Best / Liempde.

Museums: Kostuummuseum (Costumes), Noordhorn / Draaiorgelmuseum (Barrel organs), Assen / Edams Museum, Edam / Muziekinstrumentmakersmuseum (Musical instrument makers), Tilburg.

School Museums: Exmorra / Ootmarsum / Rotterdam / Burgh-Haamstede / Terneuzen.

Cheese Museums: Alkmaar / Maarsbergen / Bodegraven / Gouda.

Costume Museums: Epe / Warnsveld / Spakenburg / Huizen / Volendam / Goes / Hulst.

Chapter 9 — *The most important sights and attractions in farming, crop cultivation and livestock farming.*

Livestock Markets: Zuidlaren, Horse Market, 3rd Tuesday of October / Barneveld, Fowl Show, November / Coevorden, Goose Market, 2nd Monday of November / Purmerend, Cattle Market, regular event / Zwolle.

Fruit Areas: Betuwe / Tiel, Oogst-Fruit Corso (Fruit Harvest Pageant), September.

Bee Market: Veenendaal, 3rd Tuesday of July.

Bee Culture: Bijnstal, Hengelo / Bijenhuis, Wageningen / Bijenland, Zevenaar / Bijenschans, Hilversum / Imkerij, Grijpskerke.

Sheep Fold: Ruinen / Ede / Heinkenszand.

Duck Decoy: 't Zand.

Museums: Nationaal Rijtuigmuseum (Transport), Leek / Museum Broeker Veiling (Auctions), Broek op Langedijk / Agrarisch Streekmuseum (Regional Agriculture), Eersel / Pluimveemuseum (Poultry Museum), Barneveld / Stoomhoutzagerij (Steam Timber Mill), Groenlo / Trekkermuseum (Tractor Museum), Nisse / Veeteeltmuseum (Livestock), Beers (bij Cuyk).

Fruit Growing Museums: Kapelle / Erichem / 't Olde Ras, Doesburg.

Agriculture Museums: Dreischor / Exmorra / Veenklooster / Diepenheim / Hardenberg / Luttenberg / Bergharen / Wageningen / Hippolytushoef / Texel / Sint Anna ter Muiden / Helmond / Horst.

Chapter 10 — *The most important open-air bulbous plant locations (bloom: April and May).*

Most bulb fields are located around Noordwijkerhout, Lisse, Hillegom, between Castricum and Bergen and at the top of Noord-Holland. Also, to a lesser extent, on the Flevopolder.

Botanical Gardens: Amsterdam / Haren / Leiden / Nijmegen / Utrecht / Wageningen / Kerkrade / Steyl.

Arboreta: Doorn / De Lutte / Enschede / Rotterdam / Oudenbosch.

Museums: Bloembollenmuseum (Bulb Museum), Limmen / Museum Anna Paulowna, Anna Paulowna / Museum de zwarte Tulp (Black Tulip Museum), Lisse.

Chapter 11 — *The most important sights and attractions in ornamental plant cultivation.*

The Netherlands is one of the most important flower producing countries in the world and most gardens are well kept and bursting with flowers. The Dutch also love flowers in their homes. Dutch flower growers constantly endeavour to create new variants. There are many places where flowers and related attractions can be admired:

Annual Flower Show: Westfriese Flora, Bovenkarspel, February.

Flower Pageants: Leersum, 3rd Saturday of August / Winterswijk, last Friday and Saturday of August / Paterswolde, 1st weekend in September / Lichtenvoorde, 2nd Sunday of September / Zundert, 1st Sunday of September / Noordwijk / Vollenhove / Kindercorso (Children's Pageant), Rijnsburg, August / Bloemmozaïekdagen (Flower Mosaic Days) May, Anna Paulowna / Limmen.

Gardens and Exhibitions: Keukenhof / de Buitenhof, Lisse / Kasteeltuinen, Arcen / De Hof van Heden, Beemster / de Tuinen van Mien Ruys, Dedemsvaart / Thijsse's Hof, Bloemendaal / De Heimanshof, Hoofddorp.

Markets/Shows: Bloemenmarkt (Flower Market), Groningen, Good Friday / Krimpen a/d IJssel, June / Rozenshow (Rose Show), Broek op Langedijk, Whitsun weekend / 1st Weekend of April, 'kom naar de kas dagen' (Visit the Greenhouse Days).

Museums: Tuinbouw Museum (Horticulture), Honselersdijk / Boomkwekerijmuseum (Tree Museum), Boskoop / Broeker Veiling (Auctions), Broek op Langedijk / Museum Ter Aar, Ter Aar / Land- en Tuinbouwmuseum (Crop cultivation and horticulture), Etten-leur / Historische tuin Aalsmeer (Historical Garden), Aalsmeer.

Chapter 12 — *The most important winter events.*

Arrival of Santa Claus: 2nd and 3rd week of November, depending on municipality. December 5: 'pakjesavond' (Gift evening).

Christmas Markets: 2nd and 3rd week of December / Charles Dickens Christmas Market, Deventer.

Carnival Processions: Maastricht / Eindhoven / 's Hertogenbosch / Breda. Dates vary by municipality.

Skating Races on Natural Ice: Only during extended periods of frost.

Examples: Elfstedentocht (Eleven Cities Race), Leeuwarden, Friesland / Noorder Rondritten, Appingedam, Groningen / Toertocht op de Hunze, De Groeve, Drenthe / Siebrand / van Benthem Tocht, Bolkzijl, Overijssel / Zeewoldertocht, Zeewolde, Flevoland / Prestatietocht Oude Waal, (Ooypolder) Nijmegen, Gelderland / Toertocht Ronde van Midden-Holland, Oud-Loosdrecht, Utrecht / Molen en Merentocht (Mill and Lake Race), Krommeniedijk, Noord-Holland / Molentocht Alblasserwaard (Mill Route), Alblasserdam, Zuid-Holland / Toertocht Sluis-Brugge (Locks and Bridges), Sluis (Lock), Zeeland / Biesboschtocht, Hank, Noord-Brabant / Noordervaart Toertocht, Nederweert, Limburg

Museums: Schaatsmuseum (Ice Skate Museum), Hindeloopen / Dickens Museum, Bronkhorst / Carnavalsmuseum Oeteldonks (Carnival), 's Hertogenbosch.

A Word of Thanks

With the end result in my hand, I finally feel ready to declare that the process of conceptualising, creating and completing this book has been a successful enterprise. Moreover, I found enormous enjoyment in the process itself. Firstly, I would like to thank all those people who trusted me and posed so spontaneously and enthusiastically for an unknown photographer. In my experience, the Dutch are a friendly and helpful people, who always seem to be smiling when captured on a photograph. Without these kind people it would not have been possible to create a book such as this. I would also like to express my gratitude to all the companies and institutions that allowed me to photograph their properties. My final word of thanks goes to my closest family for their tolerance and understanding. I spent a great deal of extra time (including family time), over and above long days of photojournalism on preparations, intensive negotiations and the many other tasks that go into making a publication such as this a successful one.

The following people, companies and institutions contributed directly or indirectly to the creation of this book by providing advice, information, assistance, guidance, mediation, discounts, support, confidence, posing, etc.

K. Huyser, W.C. van Engelen, J. Hop, A.D. de Boer, J. de Bruin, W.R. Pfeiffer Jr., K. Siekmans, T. Zwijsen, E. Stegeman, J. Verhage, E. van Gerven, M. Zandee, G. van Kalsbeek.

Associations and Companies:
De Hollandsche Molen
AVN
Bikkel en Been
Bloemenbureau Holland
Staatsbosbeheer
Productschap Zuivel
Natuurpark Lelystad
K.N.S.B.
It Fryske Gea

Employees and/or Participants of:
the diverse events throughout the Netherlands
N.V. Koninklijke Delftsch Aardewerkfabriek "De Porceleyne Fles Anno 1653"
Hollands Scheepvaartmuseum, Amsterdam
Bataviawerf, Lelystad
Prehistorisch Openluchtmuseum Eindhoven
Vereniging Dorestad Sibbe
Kanonniers van Het Hollands Vestingmuseum, Naarden
Volendams Operakoor
Ons Boeregoed
Natuurmonumenten
Molen 'De Vriendschap'
Openluchtmuseum De Zaanse Schans
Keukenhof
Schilder B.V.
Cismo B.V.
Bloemenveiling Naaldwijk
Jachtvereniging Soestdijk
Charles Dickens Christmas Market, Deventer
Santa Claus and Black Peters, Super de Boer

Everyone I photographed, and everyone failed to mention by name.
Thank you!

Perfect Picture
Dirk Melchior de Boer.

Nature & Nostalgia